Brilliant Deductions

BRILLIANT
DEDUCTIONS

Wade B. Cook

Published by
Lighthouse Publishing Group, Inc.
Seattle, Washington

Distributed by
Midpoint Trade Books, Inc.

Library of Congress Cataloging-in-Publication Data

Cook, Wade B.
BRILLIANT DEDUCTIONS/Wade B. Cook
p. cm.
Includes index.
1. Income tax deductions-United States. 2. Tax
Planning-United States. I. Title.
KF6385.Z9C66 1997
343.7305'2044--dc21
97-31549
ISBN 0-910019-89-4 (cloth)

"This publication is designed to provide accurate and authorita-
tive information in regard to the subject matter covered. It is sold
with the understanding that the publisher is not engaged in
rendering legal, accounting, or other professional service, and is
not intended to take the place of such services or advice. If legal
advice or other expert assistance is required, the services of a
competent professional person should be sought."

— From a declaration of principles jointly adopted by a
committee of the American Bar Association and
committee of the Publisher's Association

Dust Jacket and Endleaf Design by Angela D. Wilson

Book Design by Judy Burkhalter

Published by
Lighthouse Publishing Group, Inc.
14675 Interurban Avenue South
Seattle, Washington 98168-4664
(206) 901-3000
fax: (206) 901-3170
www.wadecook.com
www.lighthousebooks.com
Printed in the United States of America
10 9 8 7 6 5 4 3 2

To All Believers in the American Dream

The ever-changing and time sensitive nature of the Internal Revenue Code has made it necessary for this book to be continually reviewed for accuracy. I am truly grateful for the assistance Eric Marler, Tim Berry and Stuart Stout have provided. They have spent many hours researching the tax laws, including the most recent changes, in order to provide the most up-to-the-minute information. Heartfelt thanks goes to Lighthouse Publishing Group, Inc., Cheryle Hamilton, Jerry Miller and Alison Curtis, who publish my books together with our Publications Department, Mark Engelbrecht, Angela Wilson, Connie Suehiro, Brent Magarrell, and Judy Burkhalter, who carefully edit, proof and create them. And last, but not least, a special thank you goes to my wife, Laura, for her never-ending support and encouragement.

Contents

ix   Chapter Outlines

xvi   Preface

01   Chapter One: Changing the Nature of Income

15   Chapter Two: Different Methods of Reducing Taxable Income

27   Chapter Three: How to Get Rich in Spite of the New Tax Law

41   Chapter Four: Big and Small Tax Savings

71   Chapter Five: Investment Formats

83   Chapter Six: Structuring Your Affairs

91   Chapter Seven: Corporate Strategies

109 Chapter Eight: Pension Plans

129 Chapter Nine: Living Trust Exposed

147 Chapter Ten: Transferring and Controlling

167 Chapter Eleven: Put Your Faith in Trusts

175 Chapter Twelve: Putting It All Together

189 Conclusion

193 Appendix One: Case Studies

207 Appendix Two: Legend

217 Appendix Three: Available Resources

233 Abbreviations

235 Glossary

255 Index

Chapter Outlines

01   **Chapter One: Changing The Nature of Income**
02   Financial Structuring—Wade Cook Seminars, Inc. vs. Other Professionals
07   Lower Personal Taxes
08   Municipal Bonds
11   General Annuity Income
11   Income Offset with Tax Write offs
12   Allocating Income

15   **Chapter Two: Different Methods of Reducing Taxable Income**
16   Different Tax Brackets
16   Tax Brackets for Married People Filing Jointly on Adjusted Gross Income (AGI)
17   Tax Brackets for Single People
17   Tax Brackets for "C" Corporations
19   Corporate Taxes vs. Individual Taxes
20   Income Splitting
21   Looking at Taxation From a Different Viewpoint
25   Business Tax Deductions

27   **Chapter Three: How To Get Rich in Spite of the New Tax Law**
30   New Tax Credits
33   A Few Specifics
36   Buying or Selling a Business
38   Summary

41   **Chapter Four: Big and Small Tax Savings**
42   Net Operating Loss
43   Immediate Refund
44   Go Figure
46   Corporations
46   Forms
46   How To Avoid Audits
49   Year-End Maneuvers
50   After Year End (Post December 31st) Opportunities

53   Tax Points
55   Installment Sales
59   Section 179 Internal Revenue Code

71   Chapter Five: Investment Formats
73   Cash-to-Asset-to-Cash
73   Own Your Own Business
74   Avoid Costly Entanglements
75   Law of Leverage
76   Stock Market Investors
78   The Exclusion Rule
80   Investing with Annuities
81   Maximizing the Programs Available for College Tuition

83   Chapter Six: Structuring Your Affairs
83   Tax Brackets
86   Capital Gains—Active or Passive?
86   Business Calculations
86   Double Taxation
87   Owner—Control—Income
88   Rule A
89   Rule B

91   Chapter Seven: Corporate Strategies
91   Three Aspects of Investments
92   Watch What Rich People Do
92   Sole Proprietorships
93   Why Incorporate?
95   Controlled Groups
96   Control
97   Nevada
99   Other Corporate Strategies
100   Corporations and Living Trusts
102   Corporate Year-Ends
105   October 31st Year-End

109   Chapter Eight: Pension Plans
114   How Big?
124   401(k)
126   Advantages of 401(k)

129   Chapter Nine: Living Trust Exposed
130   The Five Entities
131   What is Probate?
131   Living Trusts vs. Wills
134   What Living Trust Can and Cannot Do

147   Chapter Ten: Transferring and Controlling
147   Gifting
151   Family Limited Partnerships
156   Tax Consequences
162   Family Limited Partnership: A Comparison with
       Corporations

167   Chapter Eleven: Put Your Faith in Trusts
168   Charitable Remainder Trust
173   Trustee
174   Other Trusts—A Brief Overview

175   Chapter Twelve: Putting it All Together
175   Corporation
176   Living Trust
176   Pension Plan
177   Limited Partnerships (Family)
178   Charitable Remainder Trust
178   An Integration of Entities

Other books by Wade B. Cook:

Wall Street Money Machine

Stock Market Miracles

Bear Market Baloney

Real Estate Money Machine

How To Pick Up Foreclosures

Cook's Book On Creative Real Estate

Real Estate for Real People

101 Ways To Buy Real Estate Without Cash

Blueprints for Success (1998)

Business Buy The Bible

A+ (1998)

Don't Set Goals (The Old Way)

Wealth 101

555 Clean Jokes

Preface

"Kings ought to shear, not skin their sheep."

—*English poet Robert Herrick, shortly after the execution of Charles I, who had imposed numerous burdensome taxes on his subjects.*

Most people learn how to play games from watching someone else. Once in a while, someone has to go back and read the rules to learn how to play the game right. One of the hardest problems when trying to figure out how to legally come up with ways to pay fewer taxes, is that we usually learn the rules from people who don't have our best interests in mind. Just imagine your tax preparer going home tonight, snuggling down into bed, and pulling the covers up around his neck. Tell me, how much is he worried about your tax situation? It could be the difference between having your business stay in business or go out of business, and making a little bit of money or a lot of money. To you, it is extremely important; to him, you're just another client.

> **BUILD A FORTUNE FOR YOUR FUTURE**

One of the reasons I love this country so much is simply because we have the right to fail. I know that sounds crazy, but if you have the right to fail, you also have the right to succeed. In a country where you have the right to fail, you also have the right to build something for your future, family, or posterity.

This country breeds passion and that is the key. As you find a need and fill it, as you build and prosper in the economy, and as you use your talents and your resources to do so, you create something that was not there before, and make something bad into something good. Most of the people I have met who live this American dream find a lot of satisfaction in achieving and becoming all they can be.

This is a country where you can build a financial dynasty for your benefit and the benefit of your family. This is the greatest country in the world to accumulate wealth. Ironically, one of the saddest commentaries is that America has become a tax haven for many other people around the world. They can come here, use their money, make a lot of money, take that money back offshore and seriously minimize their taxes. However, we as American citizens have to pay extremely high taxes.

I'm going to paraphrase and then follow the lead of Ronald Reagan when he said, "If we really want to be patriotic, it's our job to keep our money at home, working and building up neighborhoods, creating jobs, beautifying this great country of ours and sending less of it to Washington, D.C. where they have mismanaged our money so greatly, without producing any new wealth." It is imperative that each one of us comes up with ways to keep the chips on our side of the table, working for us, and doing the best for us currently and in the future.

KEEP YOUR MONEY WORKING FOR YOU

BENEFITS OF OWNERSHIP

Everything I teach in regard to making money has the twist of building up cash flow. There are three primary benefits of ownership. One is the income which the ownership of assets produces. The second is tax write offs which accrue from the ownership of an asset or business. And the third benefit is the growth or appreciation which can either be accomplished by building value into an asset or business, by inflation, or by a combination of these two. One quick side point: many times investments and businesses are purchased with some kind of debt. Another type of growth or enhancement of an equity position is accomplished by retiring or reducing the debt, thereby creating "equity."

Of these three things, the need for tax write offs will go up and down. It will change from year to year. One year you'll need a lot of tax write offs; the next year you'll need very little, depending on circumstances in your life and business. Your need for growth may be really high in your middle years as you're looking forward to retirement. But the growth you need is growth of assets–which will produce cash flow in the future.

> OUR NEED FOR CASH FLOW WILL ALWAYS INCREASE

There is one thing that always goes up—your need for cash flow, your need to keep more of what you are making, your need to have that money available on a liquid basis for your use now and in the future. Your need for cash flow will increase, even as you go into retirement. If you have substantial assets, you'll need to have those assets produce income for you. We live in a monthly payment society. Most of the bills we have are on a monthly basis—our electric bills, our house and rent payments are all done on a monthly basis.

I have been teaching about the creation of perpetual monthly income for many years. When I wrote my first book, **Real Estate Money Machine**, I had no idea what a revolution it would cause in the real estate investing arena. It has been very gratifying to see so many tens of thousands of people use and implement the ideas I accidentally stumbled across. And now more than a decade later, I feel totally vindicated in all I've tried to teach.

I've seen over 140 different seminars come and go. Instructors are talking about inflation, relying on tax write offs or government programs—literally showing people how to be out of control of their money by tapping the great potential of real estate or some other investment and then sitting back and not doing any hard work to make it happen. I feel like a lone wolf because I teach exactly the opposite: build up your cash flow, avoid cost entanglements, avoid banks, avoid rentals, avoid anything that will cause you to get discouraged and quit. In other words, keep control of your money.

| MONTHLY INCOME IS THE KEY |

There are so many incredible ways of making money in this country, but the bottom line comes back to something simple—build up income. Most people do not need another job or business. What they need is income from another job or business to replace the income they have coming in right now. They need income on a monthly basis.

Today, I teach those same techniques but apply them to the stock market. I wrote **Wall Street Money Machine** and, once again, cash flow is the theme. They can have more time to dedicate to being better parents and spending more time with their children or grandchildren. They can go back to college and take courses they really want to take. They can travel and visit different parts of the world. The thing that allows all of this to happen is simply income on increased cash flow.

TAXATION

Because I have such a high profile doing radio and TV talk shows all around the country, I chose long ago to learn, implement, and use the rules of the IRS to enhance my financial position. Not to overuse a cliche—I take lemons and turn them into lemonade.

I have heard hundreds of bizarre ideas. After I do a TV or radio show or teach a seminar, somebody always tells me some farfetched idea, though some of them have a grain of sense. They always bring up some phrase in the constitution or other documents which state we do not have to pay taxes. I agree philosophically with many of these ideas and I've read about them extensively. I've read newsletters and books, and I've heard some of the greatest arguments ever, sometimes by people who have written their books in jail.

I have surveyed the whole scene and found that the people who are getting the wealthiest are the people who have assets which produce tax write offs to offset other kinds of income. So while they were growing in value, the same type of investments are also producing tax write offs. Usually these types of investments are also producing excess income. The types of investments I am talking about (rental income properties) might not be producing excess cash flow today, but more than likely they will do so in the future.

My point is, investments which produce tax write offs are the same types of investments which produce cash flow and growth. The two major areas for accomplishing this are real estate and owning your own business. If people want to learn how to get wealthy and not provoke the ire of the IRS, then it is necessary to learn the IRS rules better than the IRS. This is not hard to do because most of the people associated with the IRS are not very familiar with all the different rules, formats and legal structures that entrepreneurs have at their disposal. Therefore, you can get very wealthy and have substantial cash flow during the process. At the end of the process you'll have substantial assets built up to produce even greater cash flow. All this by using the rules, and doing everything legally within the right framework.

REAL ESTATE AND
OWNING A
BUSINESS

VISUALIZING SUCCESS

This whole process takes a lot of thought and care. Many people who promote diets say you should think about yourself in such a way that you actually picture yourself being thin—then become that type of person. This idea can be applied to the financial arena. See yourself running a grouping of different legal entities or companies that produce substantial amounts of prosperity in terms of asset enhancement and cash flow. Also see that you are able to keep a lion's share of all the profits you are making, and use these profits to continue building a nice lifestyle. In many small ways, you'll see things that you can do on a month-to-month or year-to-year basis. But more importantly, I'm hoping you'll see a whole new way of looking at your financial situation.

USE MAJOR STRUCTURING TECHNIQUES

This book is not designed to go into competition with a "fill in the blank" tax book. There are enough of those books available and I really recommend them. I've learned many good strategies from those types of books, but it's usually on how to deduct this or that. There are a few good things in those, but not major structuring ideas. What they don't contain are major structuring ideas. For example, I ordered one on tax loopholes that cost around $100. It was a huge book and I read it for any tidbit which would help me save money. I did find a few things that would get me back the cost of the book, but nothing compared to what the promotion promised.

STRUCTURING YOUR FINANCIAL AFFAIRS

I help my clients save literally tens of thousands of dollars a year by restructuring their financial affairs. I introduce a different way of looking at the accumulation of wealth in this country. I take a holistic approach to making money, investing money, and running a business.

INTEGRATE YOUR ENTITIES

Your business or other legal entities should be integrated with each other so everything works hand in hand. Then you can literally change the nature of income; you can quit having the IRS tell you when you have to claim income as income; you can move money into lower tax brackets; and you can keep control of your money and continually improve your asset base. Eventually you'll get to the point where you have not only created perpetual monthly income, but you'll have assets producing excess income which will allow you to accumulate more assets. These assets produce more monthly checks, which will buy more assets, which produce more monthly checks, and on and on.

This is the cycle you need, and my job, as the author of this book, is to guide you through the maze of all the wishy-washy information out there that does not work.

I have helped thousands of people set up Nevada Corporations, Living Trusts, and Pension Plans—and to this day, not one of these people has been audited that I know of. I am going to teach you a way of using the rules and regulations to build up a huge amount of wealth, with none of the negative side effects. This is going to become much more than just a book on deductions. As you have probably already perceived, the word deductions here could have a double meaning: it could mean deductions in taxes (which is the main thrust of this book), or it could mean deductions in the form of deducting something from something else. If one good idea comes out and is applied to one particular situation, for example a tax situation, and it is also going to produce more income or a better asset structure, then you have done well.

> NO ONE HAS
> BEEN AUDITED

The best way to make money is to not need any deductions at all. This is almost impossible with most of the money-making strategies you are employing today. As you go through the book, there are some other things you'll encounter:

1) I'm going to show you ways of building up income you won't have to claim.

2) I'll show you ways of claiming income over a long period of time, deferring in

come, keeping deductible items to off
set the income, allocating income to
other tax brackets, and claiming income
in other tax years.

All in all, the idea is to continue to build up your asset
base and income, but to not have to claim that income at any
particular time and in any particular tax bracket. With the
tax laws imposed in the early 1990s, it is imperative to learn
every different strategy we can to offset our tax liability. Within
the framework of the new tax laws there are three or four really great ideas which seem to have missed the White House's
eye for increasing taxes. I'll cover those in this book.

SUCCESS IN BUSINESS

A lot of people think the difference between a successful
business and an unsuccessful business is something gigantic. I've been around long enough to

BIG DIFFERENCES COME
FROM SMALL THINGS

realize there is not a big difference between a good
and a bad business. It could be one more customer or one more deal that makes the difference between making payroll and not making
payroll. It is the little things that add up to big
results. Wisdom, to me, is the proper application of knowledge. Successful business people apply proper business techniques. They realize their biggest single outlay is going to be
taxes—usually larger than payroll, usually larger than rent or
any other single expense. Since this is the case, anything you
can do legally to lessen the tax bite is going to be good for
your business, employees, community, and country.

We need to have fewer businesses going out of business
and more staying in business. This book is designed to teach
you the rules so you can play the game better. There is an old
Irish proverb that says, "The biggest fish you'll ever catch is
still swimming in the ocean." It is so true. The most money
you are ever going to make is still out there; the biggest deal
you're ever going to put together is still out there; the best

business you're ever going to run is still out there; the best investments you're ever going to have are still out there. So it is my job as an educator to help you get a bigger boat and better bait so you can catch that big fish.

TO WHOM ARE YOU LISTENING?

RUB SHOULDERS WITH SUCCESS

One of the problems that all of us experience is the advice we get from other people who either do not know what they are talking about or have their own agenda. Specifically, I'm talking about tax preparers. One of the questions I ask at my seminars is, "How many of you would seriously like to make over $100,000 a year?" Hands go up all over the audience, and I say to them, "If you really want to make $100,000 a year, why are you talking to anyone about making money who is making under $100,000 a year? To whom are you listening? Where are you going for your advice? If you really want to make that kind of money, then who should you be hanging around and rubbing shoulders with?"

I'll interject a quick thought about a multi-millionaire that came through my Wealth Academy. This man was worth about $2.4 million. The first day of the seminar we go around the room and everyone stands and introduces themselves. They tell who they are, where they are from and why they are taking the seminar. The multi-millionaire just stood up and said, "Hello, my name is Jim, and I'm from Las Vegas. I wanted to come here to hang around for a week with people who will spend thousands of dollars on a seminar." Everyone chuckled. Everyone thought it was funny and yet there was so much truth in what he said.

Here was a man who wanted to be around people who valued education as highly as he did. Realizing just one good idea, one good strategy, one ten thousand dollar item, implemented over and over again could make him a millionaire. It's a small price to pay to be around teachers and students who are in the mindset of making that kind of money.

The problem now is most of us do not hang around people who are making that kind of money. You may go to a seminar and hear a two million dollar idea, then go home and run it

WHY FOLLOW THEIR ADVICE?

past someone who is making $35,000 a year. The average attorney in this country makes $58,000 a year; the average real estate agent makes $19,200 a year; the average CPA makes $38,000 a year. The question is really simple. What are you listening to those people for? If they knew how to make money, they would be out making money.

Please don't get me wrong. I have a real respect for people who are constantly on the search for knowledge, but in the professional fields, I've found that once people get their license, they stagnate. They do not continue to learn and grow. I have a hard time myself going to a CPA who does not have to make payroll himself. I want to be around people who know how to make money and are faced with the same problems and concerns I'm faced with. A lot of people in this country are making more money than their tax professionals. While CPAs may do a fairly good job on bookkeeping, they will never do the extensive job needed to save more money from taxes.

CPAs—FRIENDS OR FOES?

In 1986 there was a serious change in the way relationships with tax preparing professionals were handled. At that

BIG CHANGES IN 1986

point in time, CPAs were required, in a quasi way, to work for the federal government. Tax preparers are now required to have a number from the IRS. If they stick out, cause problems, or take too much of an aggressive approach, they lose their ability to prepare taxes for people. So while you may be able to take advantage of a $200,000 savings, a CPA will not be aggressive because he wants to keep his business.

To prove this point, find out what would happen if you get audited. If you get audited, your CPA is going to get his own attorney and you're going to have to get your own attorney to go in and defend your situation. At that point in time, your CPA becomes your foe. You have to go in and literally fight this situation without their assistance on something that they may have caused.

Therefore, you don't see CPAs going into these aggressive areas and showing you the things you can do—a thing such as Section 179. (You will read about this later on.) It is so simple, but if you do not remind your CPAs or tax preparers, they will go ahead and depreciate your capital expenditures over the period of time and not take the maximum deductions you're allowed in any given year. These are not even gray areas. These are simple tax reduction strategies you could and should be using.

You literally need to take the bull by the horns in these tax situations and not rely on anyone else for your education. You need to go into book stores and get every book you can on taxation, because just as soon as we figure out the laws, they may change. You need to be talking to other business people about what they do. You need to be getting a variety of opinions from different tax preparation specialists. You need conflicting opinions to base your decision on.

YOU NEED TO KEEP STUDYING

Don't delegate this part of your business to anyone else, because the more astute you are at these sorts of things, the more you'll be able to educate your CPA about your personal situation and not have them throw you in the hopper with all the other businesses they are preparing taxes for. All you'll hear from them is, "Well, it looks like you're going to have to pay taxes on that," or "Well, you made that kind of money, that is just part of the problem with doing business in

	America—you make money, you've got to pay
YOU CAN LEGALLY AVOID SOME TAXES	taxes on it." Instead of showing you ways of moving that money around, lowering the tax brackets, or lessening the tax liability, they always say, "You'll have to pay taxes on that." You won't hear any of that here.

THE THREE FINANCIAL GOLIATHS

In this book, you'll learn good, solid approaches, not only to save money on taxes, but also on how to avoid the three different financial Goliaths: 1) lawsuits, 2) income taxes, and 3) death taxes. Look at these three things as you think of these questions, "If you make all of the money you are going to make under you, and if all of the assets you own are held under you, do you stand pretty vulnerable? Could one lawsuit wipe out everything? Do you have one income tax bracket for everything?"

SPLIT UP YOUR ASSETS

The answer to all three of these financial Goliaths is to split up your assets—to have your investments, businesses, and different equities owned in different legal entities so that one lawsuit does not affect everything you own. Do not have all of your money being made in one income tax bracket, but in several different income tax brackets. When I say split up your assets, I don't mean take everything you own and form one Nevada Corporation and put everything in there. If you make millions of dollars in one corporation, you still have the same problems. You need to split up your assets in many different ways.

As we go through this journey together of learning how to use these deductions in a brilliant format, I think you'll see yourself within the pages of this book many times. So let's get started.

Chapter One

Changing the Nature of Income

"I am proud to be paying taxes in the United States. The only thing is—I could be just as proud for half the money."

—Aurthur Godfrey

As always, there is a good and bad side to everything. I'm always looking for the silver lining in every cloud. Although there are many bad aspects to the new tax law, there are a few really good things you can take advantage of. You need to learn how to lower your tax bracket. Specifically, once you learn these methods you will be able to lower the taxes you pay by substantial amounts.

Simply put, I learned how to make a lot of money. I believe making money is the best tax shelter you could ever have. The problem is, we now (1997) have an administration in the White House that is deter-mined to get the tax rates up. Literally, without saying so, they are punishing the producers. My personal philosophy is if they want to take in more money, they should lower the tax rates. History and logic prove, if you want more of something, tax it less. If you want less of something, tax it more. If you want more profits, more productivity, more jobs, then do not tax into oblivion those things that create wealth

> MAKING MORE MONEY IS THE BEST TAX SHELTER

and jobs. As a matter of fact, if you want more, you should be lowering the tax rate. This thereby encourages people to step out, step up, and go out and make a lot of money.

FINANCIAL STRUCTURING—WADE COOK SEMINARS, INC. VS. OTHER PROFESSIONALS

A lot of people go through my Wall Street Workshop seminar. They go home and talk to their CPAs, who many times "shoot down" these great wealthbuilding ideas.

I continually refer back to the question—to whom are you listening? Where are you going for your advice? Why would you ever ask a CPA questions about the worthiness of a multi-million dollar idea or a business enterprise you want to start up? Maybe they can help you with the bookkeeping, but they do not know anything about what it takes to make a lot of money in this country. Let me give you a case in point.

> DO THEY KNOW HOW TO MAKE MONEY?

I received a phone call from a man named Roy, who has a business netting almost one million dollars per year. My company, Wade Cook Seminars, Inc., had him structured with Nevada Corporations, Limited Partnerships, and Pension Plans, which moved money down to his children. He was able to have all these taxable entities (and move money over to Nevada) so he could save on taxes. We really had him structured nicely. His CPA found one part he did not like, and pretty much tried to "shoot down" the whole structure based on one little thing.

The CPA thought there was a limit of how much money this one corporation could move over to Nevada. He thought the amount was $100,000. It would not have been difficult to have this money moved off. Setting up a Nevada corporation costs under $1,500 and it was going to save Roy $5,000 to $8,000 a year in state income taxes—a substantial amount of money. We got the CPA on the phone to do some consulting with him. He was belligerent until we convinced him we were not after bandaids. We were not trying to solve just a tax problem. There was an estate planning problem, a retirement problem, and a cash flow situation that could get eaten alive in taxes. So, with the help of our attorneys, we had totally restructured Roy's financial affairs.

> WE'RE NOT TRYING TO APPLY BANDAIDS

At one heated part of this discussion, we asked Roy's CPA why he hadn't advised his client five years ago to set up a Pension Plan. Roy should have had a pension plan all this time. If he had just put in $30,000 for the husband and $30,000 for the wife, $60,000 of deductions would have been going into an account and growing tax deferred for their retirement. Over the last five years it would have equaled $300,000, earning dividends and interest tax deferred.

Why wasn't the CPA giving the proper advice to his client, who became our client? We were trying to structure him and help him see the potential of all the different tools available for structuring his financial affairs. By following the CPA's advice, Roy pays more in taxes, has less to show for his work, and doesn't have much money for his retirement. That all changed when Roy met us.

Another time, I was talking to someone who was really excited about doing the "Money Machine" (my style of real estate) to make a lot of money. The timing was right in his life, and building cash flow was important. He had purchased our program and was ready to go. Then he talked to a CPA and real estate broker who told him, "You can't do that around here."

May I make a recommendation? When somebody tells you that you cannot do something, all they are saying is "I cannot do that something." Everything you need to create a huge amount of

> EVERYTHING IS HERE

monthly income is contained in these courses: forms, documents, places to go, people to see, things to do. We have it all here for you. You can do it.

People need to restructure themselves financially. If they are running their businesses and are already successful, or if they are just getting started, they need to set up different legal entities for managing their financial affairs. It is not a complicated process. Once you understand the different pieces of the puzzle, it is easy to put the puzzle together. But, if you don't follow our advice and instead follow the CPAs' advice, don't have a corporation, but instead own everything in one legal entity (like a husband and wife in joint tenancy), are you protected? No! Joint tenancy is one of the worst ways to own anything, because everything is taxed in one legal entity, one tax bracket. Are you protected if you go through a horrendous law suit? No, because everything is subject to one lawsuit and you could lose everything you own.

DIVERSIFICATION OF ENTITIES

What I'm talking about is not only a diversification of different investments, but also a diversification of legal entities for setting up, running, and handling your financial affairs, and controlling and owning your family's assets and businesses.

You need to minimize your tax liability and exposure to risk. This exposure is more pronounced today, especially to people who have high-profile companies, or are doctors, dentists, builders, service people, and other professionals. Until 1987, I tried to be nice to the CPAs and attorneys of the world, but it seems they just don't learn the things that can really help their customers. When a client comes to me and says, "My attorney says I don't need another corporation." I say, "Are you a corporation, Mr. Attorney? Are you a corporation, Mr. CPA? By the way, do you have a pension plan? Do you have a KEOGH plan?" They always say, "Yes." Attorneys think small business owners don't have the smarts to handle two or three different legal structures. For example, a corporation or a limited partnership to handle rental properties, another corporation for a business, another corporation for family investments, a management-type corporation set up in Nevada to move money over to avoid state taxes. Attorneys and CPAs really don't know how to integrate the functions of these entities.

PEOPLE NEED DETAILED STRUCTURING

Maybe they don't think you're capable of understanding, but I'm here to say that you are. You are the backbone of this country. You are creating the jobs. You are beautifying the neighborhoods. You are getting ready for a great retirement with your family. And you need good, solid advice.

CPAs and attorneys have difficulty dealing with entrepreneurs. They don't understand their mentality. They always look at what is, not at what could be.

You are the person who goes out and puts these ideas to work. You are the one who gets to experience the results. It is really quite simple. If you want to make a lot of money, you need to start hanging around people who will pull you up: people who bring synergy to your endeavors, people who see the whole picture, people who are not afraid to throw that bucket of cold water, but will also show a better way.

Let me tell you about a couple from Hawaii. They came through my multi-day program and were really excited about structuring their Living Trust, corporation, and partnership. This couple was worth almost $2 million. They had a few rental properties, not a lot of income, but substantial equity. They had enough income to live on and the property values were continuing to go up, so they needed some asset structuring.

Our suggestion was to have a corporation for a couple of their rental properties, and to set up a Living Trust. Even though they were in their late sixties, they still did not have enough money for their own retirement if they discontinued working. By funneling money into a retirement account, deducting the money, and not paying taxes on it right away, their retirement income would build up.

We had them all excited. They purchased a Living Trust, Pension Plan, and corporation. They then went and talked to their CPA, and not understanding how powerful a Nevada Corporation is, the CPA shot the whole idea down, and made a comment saying, "Well did you know that if you have another corporation, it is going to cost you $250 to $400 a year in bookkeeping and tax preparation charges?"

I could just see this couple say, "Oh, no, we didn't know about that. They didn't tell us about that." We were talking about helping this couple save five, ten, or fifteen thousand dollars a year (depending on how much they make). We were talking about money set aside for a great retirement, and making sure everything goes to the "stepped up" basis upon the death of one of the spouses (by using the Living Trust). We were also making sure the family kept everything and avoided probate. We had them completely structured and in just one simple comment, the whole idea got shot down. By the way, they rejected his advice and realized $250 to $400 extra a year is peanuts compared to saving $5,000 or so a year in taxes.

> USE A HOLISTIC APPROACH TO STRUCTURING YOUR AFFAIRS

In 1992, a major national newspaper did a study. They sent out tax questions to three groups of people. One group was CPAs. Another group was tax preparers you see advertised on TV. Another was the IRS—agents who should know how to fill out tax forms and answer questions.

The results were quite astonishing. The CPAs did the best, but still 60 to 72% of their answers and solutions were wrong. Do you realize what I'm saying? Close to two thirds of the advice you are given by professionals is wrong advice.

Are your attorneys and CPAs going to step up to the plate and give you advice on how to structure your affairs? Are they going to pay your taxes if you don't learn how to structure these different legal entities to lower your tax brackets? If they don't tell you how to use your children's status (like I'm going to show you) are they going to pay the extra taxes you will have to pay? If you get sued, are they going to step in and fight the lawsuit for you and the pay the amounts of money you may owe? No they are not!

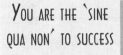

WILL THEY PAY?

You are the quarterback, coach, and coach up in the box. You are all three. Everyone is waiting for you to come on the field and make something happen. You must realize you truly arc "sinc qua non" to your success. No one should stop you with bad advice.

YOU ARE THE 'SINE QUA NON' TO SUCCESS

LOWER PERSONAL TAXES

There are many ways to receive money, but the trick is to not have to claim that money as income. One way to do that, especially if you are going to play the stock market, is to not own stocks in your own personal name. Stocks in the stock market should be owned in an IRA, some other type of retirement account, or a corporate account. I'll show you why.

If your corporation owns stock in the stock market and it receives a dividend, the corporation does not have to claim 70% of that dividend (whether it's a common stock dividend or preferred stock dividend). This is called the 70% exclusion rule. All you have to claim is 30%. For example, you have a lot of stocks in a corporate account and you build up quite a substantial portfolio over ten or fifteen years. You buy and sell some stocks, you keep some and they grow in value. Maybe they are not paying any dividends today, but they will in the future. Let's say you receive a $10,000 dividend check for one year. This is not unheard

70% EXCLUSION RULE

of if you have $100,000 to $200,000 worth of stock. Now, look at your tax brackets. It adds to your income and throws you over your $50,000 a year, or even over $75,000. All of sudden you are in a 25 to 34% tax bracket. All you have to claim is 30% of that or $3,000. The other $7,000 is ignored. If, for instance, you're in a 15% tax bracket, 15% of $3,000 is $450, as opposed to 15% of $10,000 which is $1,500. This corporate dividend exclusion is really quite exciting and is one of the better reasons for having a corporation.

MUNICIPAL BONDS

Another source of income which does not have to be considered income is that from municipal bonds. I find a lot of value in high-grade municipal bonds, especially ones that have nice large payouts. You can even

BONDS

structure the purchases of these municipal bonds so that your interest payments come at different times. You can literally support yourself, from quarter to quarter, or month to month, with these interest payments.

How would you like to accumulate $300,000 to $500,000 worth of these high grade municipal bonds over the next 10 or 20 years? Even if they are only paying an average 5 to 6% per year, (6% of $400,000 is $24,000), it would be income without any tax consequences. Once again, you have income without having to claim it as income.

Wouldn't it be nice to have monthly income that did not have any tax implications? Wouldn't it be nice to look forward to a great retirement with extra income, which did not have to be claimed for tax purposes?

TAX-FREE

INCOME

Wouldn't it be nice for your children to be making good money—enough to support them through college and receive income without any tax ramifications?

There aren't many investment vehicles available to produce this type of "no tax consequence" income, but one is a municipal bond. There two types of city or municipal bonds:

1) *Performance Bond.* This bond has collateral and a specific structure as a payback source.

2) *General Revenue Bond.* Against the city in general. A city, to a limited extent, has the ability to raise money through increased taxation. They may also raise money through decreased taxation to generate more productivity.

Politicians do owe their allegiance to the citizenry. If they create debt against the city itself, that debt should be done in the most favorable manner possible. They cannot pay the same interest rates and cannot compete with other people who were obtaining debt. The federal government has given a special dispensation to cities, wherein the interest paid to investors would not have to be claimed for federal income tax purposes.

If you were to buy a municipal bond for any given city in the United States, you would receive quarterly, semi-annual, or annual payouts of interest income which is received tax free. You could also buy bonds at different prices and make money in that manner, depending on the rate for any given day. You could buy the bond at a lower price or at its face value. That "gain," as income, is not taxable. A word of advice: if you're in a high tax bracket and you want to have a small amount of risk associated with your investments, you could buy "AA" rated municipal bonds. You could receive these from any stock brokerage source. If you want to minimize your risk, you can also spread out your investments by buying municipal mutual fund bonds and letting professional managers take care of the portfolio for you. If you want to invest on your own, there is one other thing you should consider: if you live in a state that has state income tax, many of these states have given a second advantage of investing in municipal bonds.

If you are a resident of California and you buy California city municipal bonds, not only is it federal income tax free to you, it is now state income tax free. Some municipalities that have city income tax, for example New York, have a triple tax free municipal bond which would be free from federal, state, and city income tax. This would substantially increase the yield (which is the point of buying these municipal bonds). They only have to pay a small interest rate. If you're in a 28 or 31% tax bracket, the interest rate you are receiving is proportionately higher, simply because you do not have to pay taxes on that money.

SOMETIMES TRIPLE TAX FREE

You can also purchase these municipal bonds so the interest payouts fall due at different points in time. You could keep your cash flow not only perpetual, but also coming in on a regular and timely basis so you can meet your financial obligations.

ZERO COUPON BONDS

Some municipalities also have zero coupon municipal bonds, which means there is no interest payout until some time in the future. All the interest paid out is tax free. You can buy these municipal bonds at a substantial discount (sometimes pennies on the dollar) that will grow to maturity in future years.

Some people own municipal bonds within their IRAs or Pension Plans. I don't see any big advantage of doing this. Why would you want to buy a tax shelter-type investment within a tax shelter? If the rate of returns are good, then go ahead. You would want to own these bonds under a corporation or under yourself.

These municipal bonds are also beneficial for teenage children. If you are satisfied with the rate of return in the 6 to 9% range, these are great vehicles for building up income for your children so they can go to college.

GENERAL ANNUITY INCOME

The next type of income we'll discuss is income or gains you receive, but can spread out claiming over a long period of time (for further explanation see the Installment Sales section of Chapter Four). You can buy something at one price and sell it at another price, make a profit, and then claim that profit as you receive it.

Another type of income is in investments you defer. With this type of income, there are several points to consider. General annuity-type income is made by buying investments now. The only problem is these investments are usually made with after-tax money, unless they're made by a Pension Plan or retirement account. You can put the money into these different products, and then have it paid out fifteen or twenty years down the road in a monthly or quarterly payout program.

INCOME OFFSET WITH TAX WRITE OFFS

Another type of income is income that can be offset with other tax write offs.

1) In a business setting this is quite easy. You have income that comes in at different points in time and expenses that are paid out at different points in time. To some extent you can control the flow.

OFFSET INCOME WITH TAX WRITE OFFS

2) You can have depreciation expense or other paper-type write offs (for further explanation see the BEST workshop). Up until now you have been able to deduct a certain amount of your active income with paper write offs from rental real estate. If you meet certain criteria you can deduct all of that. This means you can make up to $150,000 or even $250,000

a year, and if you have substantial amounts of paper write offs, you could write it all off and literally take your income back down to zero. More specifically, you could take your tax bracket back down a few notches and pay substantially less.

3)   With the new availability of an active and passive way of investing in low-income housing credits, you could take advantage of this tremendous opportunity of building up tax credits. Meaning, even though you have a net income, and a tax liability, you could have credits that directly offset this tax liability. This is the best of all worlds—to have an investment growing in value and producing cash flow, giving you some depreciation and tax write offs, yet, at the same time, producing credits that are applied directly, dollar for dollar.

BUILD UP TAX CREDITS

ALLOCATING INCOME
Income you receive can be allocated to other tax brackets:

1)   Have investments owned directly by your children. The first $500 of income made by children is not taxable at all. Until the age of 14, children's tax brackets are the same as the parents. If we can keep the parents in a lower tax bracket, the monies made by the children is taxed in a lower tax bracket.

2)   Convert earned income (which is also susceptible to social security taxes). Lower income by having that income made either through an "S" Corporation or a Limited Partnership.

3)   Make money in a state that has lower taxes or no taxes at all, such as Nevada.

NEVADA—A GREAT STATE TO INCORPORATE IN

4)   Use multiple methods—not only to diversify into different kinds of investments, but also to diversify into different entities that have a variety of different investments. Use the multiple entities approach.

5) Move income made in one year to different tax tiers by having a January 31 or March 31 year-end. You get a longer period of time with the income made, which gives you a longer period of time to:

  a) Offset it with other tax deductible items.

  b) Have the money expensed out so you pay fewer taxes.

  c) Have the money available for use over a longer period of time and then pay taxes on it when the taxes are due.

In conclusion, the greatest advantage we have is realizing this is a multiple choice situation. As you look at the preceding information, realize that each one of those ways is available at any given time for your various entities—not only for you to have these different types of income, but for each one of your different entities to have these types of income at different points in time. Couple this with the fact that you can choose the type of tax structured entity you want, such as in an "S" or "C" Corporation or a Family Limited Partnership. You can control whether the money is taxed at the entity level or at the personal level. You can decide whether the money can or should be moved from one year to the next. You will see the different strategies you have available.

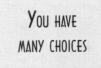

YOU HAVE MANY CHOICES

Chapter Two

Different Methods of Reducing Taxable Income

"The greater the number of statutes, the greater the number of thieves and brigands."

—*Lao Tse*

The purpose of this chapter is to show you techniques to reduce your tax bite. Paradoxically, most people want to reduce taxes as they are actually increasing their real income. It can be done if you use some or all of the following strategies.

Let me briefly mention one type of income which I'll cover extensively in the section on Family Limited Partnerships. If you have units (like stock) in your own Family Limited Partnership, at the end of the year the profits are allocated down to the respective, individual unit holders of the partnership.

For example, if you own 5% of the units, at the end of the year you'll have to claim 5% of the profits or deduct 5% of the losses of the partnership. A partnership in this manner does not have taxation to itself. The taxation is passed on to the unit holders by their percentage of ownership. This partnership could pay you a salary for managing it. That would be earned income and that income would be subject to social security taxes. However, at the end of the year,

No taxation at Partnership level

the partnership pays out to the unit holders the profits from all its activities and investments (which could be only 5% to you, as well as 40% to each of your children; or even 15% to someone else). It is calculated on a K1 or partnership return, which is then entered on your 1040. It is not earned income and therefore not subject to social security taxes. *[Note: many times the money is not paid directly to the children but goes to the family and is accounted to the children as a bank entry.]*

DIFFERENT TAX BRACKETS

I realize it's distasteful to have to pay up to 40% to the federal government and have state and local taxes on top of that. The total could reach 50% or even more. For some people, over half of the hard-earned money they make is going to go to some government.

> NO ONE WANTS TO PAY 50% TO THE GOVERNMENT

"Let's go into partnership together and here's how it will work: you take all of the risk; I'll take none of the risk; you put up all the money; I put up none of the money; you run the company on a day-to-day basis; I have nothing to do with the operation of the company. If the company fails, you pay all the bills and have all the exposure; but if the company makes a profit, I get 50% of it and you get 50%." None of us, in our right minds, would ever enter into such a partnership arrangement with anyone else. However, this is the arrangement we have with the government.

We need to be smarter than they are. We need to figure out ways of minimizing the amount of money which is subject to taxation, and we need to make it the lowest possible tax bracket available to us.

TAX BRACKETS FOR MARRIED PEOPLE FILING JOINTLY ON ADJUSTED GROSS INCOME (AGI) 1997

$0–$41,200	15%
$41,200–$99,600	28%
$99,600–$151,750	31%
$151,750–$271,050	36%

Anything over $271,050 has a 10% surcharge on highest previous bracket (36%) = 3.6%. Add that on this surcharge to everything over $271,050 and you have a 39.6% bracket.

THE BRACKET
CREEPS UP

TAX BRACKETS FOR SINGLE PEOPLE

$0–$24,650	15%
$24,650–$59,750	28%
$59,750–$124,650	31%
$124,650–$271,050	36%
$271,050 +	39.6%

(NOTE: these brackets increase slightly from year to year because of inflation adjusting.)

Before I list the corporate tax brackets, I'd like to mention the word "marginal," in relationship to your marginal tax bracket. A lot of business decisions are made on what the tax implication is going to be. If a company or person is making "X" number of dollars and calculate that they are in a 28% tax bracket, then the marginal tax bracket is simply calculated by asking yourself, "If I make one more dollar, what are the tax implications going to be?" If that comes out to 28%, then your marginal tax bracket is 28%. If that extra money is large and moves you up a bracket or two, then your marginal rate could be 31 or 36%. The tax implications we'll discuss throughout this book and the tax and business strategies we'll employ are going to be weighed against the risks. If one of these risks involves taxes on profits made, it may determine whether you want to go ahead with the enterprise or not.

THE TAX ON THE NEXT
DOLLAR COULD MAKE
A BIG DIFFERENCE

TAX BRACKETS FOR "C" CORPORATIONS

Let's go over the taxes on corporations. We're specifically talking about "C" Corporations which have their own tax brackets and are taxed at the corporate level. "S" Corporations are taxed more like a partnership and do not pay taxes in and of themselves. In "S" Corporations, tax ramifications are passed down to the individual shareholders (For further explanation on the differences between "S" and "C" Corporations see Chapter Seven).

Here are the brackets for a "C" Corporation:

$0–$50,000	15%
$50,000–$75,000	25%
$75,000–$100,000	34%
$100,000–$335,000	39%
$335,000–$10,000,000*	34%

Over $10 million of net income is taxed at 35%. (There are some exceptions to this, which if you fall over $10 million dollars—see your CPA.) There will be an additional 3% tax on any corporate income over $15 million; but only up to a $100,000 limit.

Just for fun, it is good to see the rationale behind some of these different brackets and surcharges. Specifically, I'm talking about that 5% difference between 34 and 39%. When your corporation is making small amounts of money (under $50,000, $75,000 or $100,000) tax brackets are substantially lower than your individual tax brackets. Once a corporation starts making good money, the government tacks on a 5% surcharge which makes up for what they did not collect on the lower amounts of money. The difference between the 15% and 34%, and the 25% and 34% equals this 5% difference between $100,000 and $350,000. To put this another way, when it's all said and done and you're making really big money with your corporation, then you are effectively in a 34% tax bracket on everything you're making.

THE 5% SURCHARGE MAKE-UP STRATEGY

However, there is very strong case to be made for making money under a corporation. The best way to see this is to go back and put the corporation chart over the individual chart and run the numbers right next to each other so you can see how this works. After looking at this chart, look down at the lower amount of money. You'll see that an individual is up to 28% at around $41,200, and a corporation goes to 25% at the $50,000 range. So it would be much better to make money as a corporation, rather than as an individual.

Let's put the corporate tax rates with the rate for a married couple so you can see.

Couple	$0–$41,200	15%
Corporate	*$0–$50,000*	*15%*
Couple	$41,200–$99,600	28%
Corporate	*$50,000–$75,000*	*25%*
Couple	$99,600–$151,750	31%
Corporate	*$75,000–$100,000*	*34%*
Couple	$151,750–$271,050	36%
Corporate	*$100,000–$335,000*	*39%*
Couple	$271,050–over	39.6%
Corporate	*$335,000–$10,000,000*	*34%*

CORPORATE TAXES VS. INDIVIDUAL TAXES

There have not been many times in the history of the USA when corporate taxes have been lower than individual taxes. Usually corporate taxes are substantially higher. Therefore it is better today to make money as a corporation than as an individual. If you've ever thought about being in business, this is the time to do so, and do so as a corporation. If you have to pay taxes at the end of the year, the corporation will be taxed at a corporate level and not at your level.

You could effectively make around $50,000 a year and pull out $25,000 to yourself for running the corporation. That money is going to be taxed at 15%. The other $25,000 of net profit left in the corporation is also going to be taxed at 15%. You've effectively saved 13% of $8,800 (remember $0 to $41,200 is taxed at 15%), compared to making all this money in a sole proprietorship, wherein it would all be taxed down to one person at 15 to 36%.

Corporate tax rates will save you money

When you realize the tax implications of these preceding charts, you'll realize the game is afoot. It is a matter of creating several different legal structures to keep all your tax brackets low.

Income Splitting

One of the greatest avenues of tax preparation was the avenue of income splitting. For many years, this primarily involved using children or grandchildren. It worked by allocating earned income down to their particular tax brackets. For example, parents would buy investments in the names of their children and have their children make money. More often than not, the children never saw one dime of this money. It was either kept in the account or allocated to them in a book entry and the money was used by the family to pay bills, et cetera.

The two primary methods for splitting income and reducing taxes were: 1) the purchase of investments and the earning of income in the child's tax bracket; and 2) different forms of ownership of business enterprises, such as corporations or Limited Partnerships, where the children own part of the business (even though they were too young to work in the business, the money from the business was allocated—not paid— but allocated to them in their tax brackets).

It's quite simple to see that if Mom and Dad are working and making good money and they're in a 28, 31, and 36% tax bracket, a large amount of money could be made nominally by the children and taxed in their tax brackets (15%.) Some of the income might even be taxed at 0%, and the family would be substantially better off, saving 13 to 21%.

The tax implications are minimal, if we're talking about just $5,000 to $10,000. But if we're talking about hundreds of thousands of dollars in income, then this 15 to 20% in extra taxes could represent $15,000 to $40,000. This is money that we would rather not send to Washington, D.C. A lot of people would rather have the asset base and ownership growing for their children, especially if they are controlling the investments and all the income.

This was all taken away in 1986. The law simply stated that from now on, all income made by the children is to be taxed at the same rate as their parents. When that law came out, I saw hands go up all over the country. Every tax preparer said, "There goes that one, that was sure fun while it lasted. That great avenue of allocating different income to our children has been done away with. Woe is me." They literally had their clients start paying tens of thousands of dollars in taxes to the IRS. I don't give up on a good idea, if it is truly a good idea. I keep finessing it until I come up a new way of working it. Remember the law says that from now on, all income to children under 14 years of age is taxed in the same income bracket as the parents.

> **ALWAYS STICK WITH A GOOD IDEA**

LOOKING AT TAXATION FROM A DIFFERENT VIEWPOINT

Sometimes the best way to look at something is to look at it in reverse. For example, when I was setting up my own records, I saw many different computer software programs that didn't make a lot of sense to me. It seemed they did not know what I needed the information for as a business owner. I needed good, solid information to make decisions and I needed that same information to transfer to my Schedule C or Form 1120 (for corporate taxes.) It seemed the best way to come up with a bookkeeping system was to start with the tax forms I was going to use and work backwards from there.

Let's think about children's taxation backwards. If the law says from now on the children's income for children under 14 years of age is going to be taxed at the same tax bracket as the parents, then let's look at the parents' tax brackets and try to make it smaller. This was the solution. I've taught seminars since 1986 to tax preparers and professionals from all over the country. Their mouths gape open when they see their client's tax situation in this light, and realize what they missed.

Life is not that complicated to me. Being a former cab driver, I learned a lot of simple things. Specifically, I learned that the money is in the "meter drop." The "big money" is not made by making a killing on every run, but in trying to make as many runs as possible. The huge success you'll have will not be made by trying to make a killing on any one deal, but by thinking big on a whole bunch of bite-sized pieces.

Let's go back to the parents' tax brackets. Life, once again, is not that complicated. Why not just get the parents' tax brackets down to 15%? The simple way to do that would be to have the children make all the money and have the parents not make any money. How do you do that if the parents need the money to live on? Again, the emphasis is "allocated to the children," not received by the children. This could be done as a book entry on a limited partnership form. The money is paid out to the parents for the children, but the parents receive this money. It is unearned income for the children. The parents put it in their own checking accounts and pay the bills.

> **GET THE PARENTS' TAX BRACKET DOWN TO 15%**

Here is a specific example. Let's say you have a nice business and you're making $50,000 to $100,000 a year. In the next year or two you see yourself making $100,000 to $200,000. If you make $200,000 and you're married, filing jointly you could see very quickly that a lot of the money is going to be taxed at 15, 28, and some at 31%. I am going to assume you have some money in tax deductions from interest on your home and donations to your charities or church. You have tax deductions of $40,000, but you still have taxable income of $160,000.

EXAMPLE A

Mom and Dad's income	$200,000	
minus	40,000	= Itemized Deductions
	$160,000	= Net Taxable Income

Taxes due $ 42,905

Let's do it differently this time. The business is set up as an "S" corporation or a Family Limited Partnership (ownership in this partnership is called "units" and therefore, instead of having shareholders and stockholders, we have unit holders).

Let's say you have three children, *[Note: this works for children over 14. If your children are younger than 14, their income is aggregated with that of their parents.]* allocate to the Mom 5% of the units and allocate to the Dad 5% of the units. There are 100,000 units available: 5,000 to Mom and 5,000 to Dad. Let's give each one of your kids 30% or 30,000 units. All the units are held by the three children and the two parents. The parents, through a corporation structure, are the general partners (For further explanation see Limited Partnerships in Chapter Ten). The partnership receives income and the general partner can pull out different fees and salaries for managing the affairs of the partnership. Remember these fees are not only subject to federal taxes, but also to Social Security taxes. Because of this, they do not pull out a substantial amount of money. The huge bulk of the income is left within the partnership or "S" Corporation.

HOW TO USE YOUR CHILDREN

At the end of the year, when calculating taxes, they are not calculated at the partnership level but down to the individual unit holder's level by the respective percentages of ownership. In our example, Mom and Dad owned 5% each. So 5% of $200,000 is $10,000 for each, which equals $20,000. Remember, they are filing jointly. So filing jointly at $20,000, the money is taxed at 15%. Thirty percent of this money is allocated to each of the three children—30% of $200,000 is $60,000 each.

Now go back and look at the individual tax rates for a single person and you'll realize that if a single person makes this kind of money, some of it will be taxed at 15%, and some at 28%. Anything over $59,750 is going to be taxed at 31%. The children would have to pay "X" number of dollars if they were receiving that kind of money as single children. Remember, the tax law says that all income made by children over 14 is taxed in their own tax bracket, not in the parents. The parents are at 28 to 31% and the children are now taxed at the 15% level, even though they didn't receive any of the money (it was allocated to their tax brackets). The $60,000 is divided as follows: the first $24,650 is taxed at 15%; $24,650 to $59,750 at 28%; the remaining $250 is taxed at 31%. You just saved a huge amount of money with this one example. This does not even take into account that you could still have other entities making different kinds of income and moving money from one year to the next. You can also have these entities buying things for the executives and managers, and the corporation or partnership can deduct these different business expenses.

DEDUCT MORE EXPENSE

I think you'll see the power of this as you go through some other examples in this book. You'll realize how this can be used in conjunction with the other entities and how dynamically powerful this is for lowering your tax brackets. If you don't have any children, you could have different entities owning the units; you could give away some of the units to different charities, especially after you pass away; you could use grandchildren, nieces or nephews and you could even use your parents who may be in lower tax brackets.

I know of several people who allocate certain amounts of money to their mother and father in their 70s and 80s. Sometimes their parents receive the money and sometimes they don't. Even if they don't receive the money, their children give them enough money each year to pay the taxes due on that amount of money allocated to them. This is just another way of getting everything taxed down to a 15% tax bracket.

HELP YOUR PARENTS RETIRE BETTER

I know people would really like to zero out on their taxes and not pay money in income taxes—all legally within the tax code. There are several ways of doing this which we'll cover in the items from the new tax law items.

BUSINESS TAX DEDUCTIONS

Most of you who are running your own businesses need to quit acting like an employee. I think we need to lose that employee mentality from both a success point of view and a tax point of view. Let me get more specific. Most people like to go to basketball games and football games, have nice clothes, et cetera. Did you know that seminars, books, and tapes purchased for investment purposes are no longer tax deductible? Yet books and tapes purchased for business improvement, or enhancing your business enterprise are tax deductible. This book you are now holding in your hands, if purchased for investment purposes, is not deductible. If it was purchased by your business for business purposes, it is tax deductible. If you want to go to a seminar in Hawaii for business purposes a substantial part of that trip can be deducted.

QUIT ACTING LIKE AN EMPLOYEE

Let's go back to this whole thought in general: you need to quit acting like an employee. Specifically, you need to quit spending "after-tax money." Most people, as employees, take home a pay check from their business and then go to a basketball game, buy a car, et cetera. If you have the business buy the car for you, a substantial part of the expense for buying the car could be deducted as a business expense. If you went down the list of businesses which have purchased season tickets to the L.A. Lakers or Boston Celtics, you'll see that a lot of the season ticket holders are corporations. Employee benefits can also be paid for by the corporation with "before-tax money." These can all be deductions from the net income and a reduction of the net profits of your company. *[Note: the Revenue Reform Act of 1993 reduced the deduction on meals and entertainment deductions from 80% to 50% of the gross amount spent.]*

If your small business is making $50,000 and had an additional $5,000 in expenses of this nature for enhancing your business enterprise, then $5,000 is deducted and you're making $45,000 instead of $50,000—you've saved a substantial amount of money in income taxes and Social Security taxes.

DEDUCT A TRIP TO HAWAII

Ask yourself an important question—do executives of large corporations go golfing? Do they take business trips? Do they have perks when traveling which are deducted as an expense to the company? The answer is an emphatic "yes!" Then why not learn what major corporate executives do and copy them? Have your company pay for that business trip in Hawaii and let your corporation pay for some of the things as a deduction. Again, we are changing the nature of some of the income received in this business by expensing it out.

Chapter Three

How To Get Rich In Spite of the New Tax Law

"Taxation must not take from individuals what rightfully belongs to individuals."

—*Henry George*

For many years, we have been limited in the amount of deductions, depreciation expense, and other losses, that we could take from rental real estate activities against our active income, earned income, or other kinds of business income (small business, farming, et cetera). Many years ago, we could make hundreds of thousands of dollars, even millions of dollars with our businesses, and we could buy enough tax-sheltered investments (either through limited partnerships, or through actual ownership) to take these paper losses and write off our active income. Anybody over the age of 30 should remember those years. Congress cut back these write offs so drastically that they really hurt real estate.

THE OLD LAW WAS NICE

Congress divided the two kinds of money-making endeavors into two parts. One is called "active" and the other "passive." Under the active category we had our wages, salaries, and tips. It is earned income. Dividends are active. Also

ACTIVE AND PASSIVE

included are business income, interest income, and farming income. (You can find a complete list in the booklet that goes along with Form 1040.)

Under the passive category are Limited Partnerships and rental real estate. Now people will say, "That's not true. I'm an active owner. I buy properties." That may be true, but all rental real estate is considered passive. However, if you were considered an active owner of houses, duplexes, et cetera (meaning you own more than 10% of the property and you are involved in the major decisions), you could then write off up to $25,000 of these losses against your active income. ($12,500 per year for married filing separately.) By the way, at $27^1/2$ years straight depreciation, it takes several properties to come up with those kinds of losses.

If you are making $80,000 a year, you could take up to $25,000 of these losses and offset part of the $80,000. You would then have income of $55,000. (This is a tax savings of approximately $6,000 to $7,000).

By the way, the IRS even fades out this $25,000. Once your adjusted gross income is $100,000, for every one dollar you make over the $100,000, you lose the right to write off 50¢. By the time you earn from $100,000 to $150,000, you will have wiped out your ability to use that $25,000 as a deduction this year. One dollar wipes out 50¢, so $50,000 has wiped out $25,000. Think about this. Just when you start making good money, just when you really need the write offs, they phase it away. This is the law as it exists today. The right to use these deductions to offset your income seriously limits your ability to zero out. This is why real estate has been hurt so badly in the last few years—they have taken away accelerated tax write offs. It is really hard to get cash flow with real estate. The unassumability of loans has made it really tough to buy many properties. We really have to look harder to find the proper-

JUST WHEN YOU NEED WRITE OFFS

ties which are assumable. Congress has really made real estate an unpleasant experience for a lot of people. They have turned their backs on investors who are trying to build up the economy.

But Congress and the IRS have changed the rules regarding real estate again. It is not complicated at all. Beginning in 1994, if you are in the real estate business—which means buying and selling real estate, remodeling, developing, being an agent, property management, handling rental properties and so on— and you spend at least half of your time doing it, then you can deduct all of your losses. This means you may once again zero out—if you make $80,000 and have $80,000 in losses, you have no income tax due. Half, or a minimum of 50%, of your time must be spent at your real estate enterprise to qualify for this.

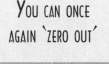
YOU CAN ONCE AGAIN `ZERO OUT`

In regard to husbands and wives, if the husband has a full-time career or full-time business, and the wife is handling the houses and other aspects of the rental property business—half or 50% of her time will mean they'll be able to take all of the losses and offset both of their incomes. One spouse will qualify them if you read it right. Both incomes can go to zero.

A corporation that has all kinds of deductions—salaries, wages, and other expenses can take all of its tax write offs against its income. From a philosophical point of view, this is really exciting. With your corporation, or as an individual, you can go out once again with your corporation or as an individual and you can make $100,000, $200,000, or $300,000 a year, buy enough of these tax-sheltered type investments, and offset your income. No matter what part of the real estate industry you're participating in, all of these losses are deductible if you meet these minimum requirements.

DEDUCT ALL YOUR LOSSES

The next item gets even more exciting than this last one. It is a new way to write off taxes that will help many people make a lot of money. With real estate we get the cash flow, tax write offs, and growth. The great thing about real estate is that you can get all three of these benefits with the same money. The same dollar that buys you cash flow is the same dollar that buys you growth. You don't need 100 cents on the dollar to do this. You can buy a $100,000 property for $5,000 or $10,000 down. You can use the law of leverage. You get the growth on the whole $100,000, not on your $10,000 down payment. You get the income on your $100,000, not on your $10,000 down payment. You get the tax write offs on the $100,000, minus the cost of land, not your $10,000.

I personally believe, if you use the tax codes like they are written and you learn them and study them, you can get very wealthy. You see, the same property you are purchasing for tax write offs (that may be your primary motive in getting this property) will also produce growth for you. A $5,000 or $10,000 down payment on a $100,000 property is producing write offs and is growing in value, and even though it is producing paper losses, it may be producing real cash flow for you. You can literally take income home every month and not have to claim it because this property has enough tax write offs to not only offset the income it is producing but to offset other income. The properties and investments we use to help our tax situation are the same investments that are growing in value and producing income.

NEW TAX CREDITS

This next item is really exciting. You may get bogged down with technicalities, but I will give you enough information to decide whether this program is for you. This is not an easy thing to do. I think everyone understands that when you are dancing with the government, you are dancing with a gorilla.

Section 42 of the Internal Revenue Code deals with low income housing credits. Do not get turned off by the word "low income." I'll explain what that means later. This is not about Section 8 or a HUD program, a program that was instituted in 1986.

For many years I traveled all over the country teaching seminars on these low income housing credits. I was responsible, like many investors, for going out and getting credits from California to Florida. These credits were dollar-for-dollar write offs against a person's tax liability. I'm aware that most of you know this, but just so that we are all on the same footing, I'll explain what this means.

LOW INCOME
HOUSING CREDITS

A deduction is subtracted from your income. If you are making $80,000, and you can come up with $10,000 worth of tax write offs, you can report $70,000 instead of $80,000. Your taxes on that $70,000 are going to be around $15,000. How would you like to directly lower the $15,000 due instead of lowering the $80,000? That is credit. There are many kinds of credits available. Most of them like research, energy, and fuel credits (for the average investor) are really hard to obtain. This one is a little difficult, but it is phenomenal.

Before June 30, 1992, you could buy rental real estate—a house, a duplex, or a 200 unit apartment building. Each state was allocated so much credit—$1.25 for every person living in a state. If you have a state with three million people, you just multiply that by $1.25 and your state would have three plus million dollars worth of these credits available. Investors would apply for these credits and get their buildings approved for use in this program.

If you purchase a "new" property you would receive a 70% tax credit. Let me explain what this means. In other words, let's say you spent $400,000 for an eight-plex. These eight units

70% TAX CREDIT FOR
NEW PROPERTY

now give you a 70% tax credit. Seventy percent of $400,000 is $280,000. You will receive this amount as a tax credit spread out over 10 years.

If you have a qualifying property at the end of this year, you could start the tax credits this year, or you could elect to delay one year and start the tax credits next year. You are going to receive one-tenth of that, or a $28,000 tax credit. If you are making $150,000 to $200,000 a year and realize you have to pay around $40,000, this large tax credit will be welcome relief. This one property will produce better results than several buildings would produce if you were just going after write offs. Let's say you make $150,000. This eight-plex will produce depreciation expense, which you may also take. If, for instance, the depreciation expense on it is about $10,000 a year (taking out the land), instead of making $150,000 a year, you are now making $140,000. This $10,000 deduction saves you almost $4,000. Now, even though you've lowered your tax liability from $40,000 to $36,000, how would you like to have this building producing a $28,000 tax credit for you? You apply the tax credit ($28,000) right against the $36,000 and all of a sudden you have an $8,000 tax liability. Simply put, you have a dollar-for-dollar tax credit right against your tax liability. There are limitations to how much you and/or your corporation can write off—see your tax professional to figure this out. Also note, this tax credit is available for the next nine years after you qualify the building.

THE BUILDING ALSO PRODUCES TAX DEDUCTIONS

Most of you won't buy a new building—you will buy used properties. If you buy a used property that is used as residential real estate right now, the credit goes from 70% down to 30%.

Let's go back through the numbers. You purchase this property for $400,000, and you receive a 30% tax credit. The 30% tax credit on $400,000 is $120,000. Once again, you spread it out over 10 years, you divide by 10 years and you get $12,000 a year. If you want more tax credits, you would have to buy more properties. Hopefully, the properties will also produce cash flow, growth, tax deductions and now these incredible tax credits.

30% CREDIT FOR USED PROPERTY

A FEW SPECIFICS

A property is considered "new" when it is newly built and has never been used before as residential real estate. Let's say you buy a warehouse and convert it into an apartment building. Obviously, this is not a new building but it has been substantially renovated. It can now qualify as a new building and get the 70% tax credit.

What qualifies a building? The median family income in your neighborhood is what is used to qualify a building. It is either done on a per unit or square footage basis on this eightplex. If 15 out of 20 tenants qualify, you would receive $^{15}/_{20}$, or $^{3}/_{4}$ of the credit.

To qualify the building, 20% of the tenants living in your units have to make 50% or less of the median family income, or 40% of your renters have to be making 60% or less of the median family income.

QUALIFICATIONS FOR THE CREDITS

If we go back to our example, you will now receive 75% (15 out of 20) of the $280,000 tax credit. Let's say you are going to try to get all of your renters in this apartment complex to qualify the building. If the median family income in your area is $34,000, you need at least 20% of the renters making $17,000 a year or less to qualify this building. The square footage percentage or unit percentage will determine how much of the tax credit you can use. The tax credit stays the same for the ten years. How much you can use each year depends on the percentage that year.

You know you cannot discriminate against people for race, creed, sex, religion, et cetera. You can discriminate against people for their financial situation. For example, if you are doing a credit report on some people, you would say, "I'm sorry, you have bad credit," or "I'm sorry, you are not making enough money, you cannot live here." Now you have to discriminate against people based on their income because you need to have people in your property who will qualify under the aforementioned rule (making less than the median family income).

You need people who qualify

The Internal Revenue Service contracts with a state agency (it differs from state to state). It is in charge of distributing, managing, and handling these tax credits. Once they are gone for the year, they are gone. You can find your state agency by calling HUD, or the IRS in your area. Once you find out who is handling the distribution and management of tax credits for your area, you will have to start jumping through some hoops.

Many states have come up with other programs to help people. For example, you can use, fund, and build these kinds of properties. They have different bonds and debt financing programs available to investors for putting these low income housing units into play. This has been a very popular program with the U.S. Congress. It has created a lot of low income housing units all over the country. You have to own the property for fifteen years. You can find a qualified buyer after the ten-year period, but you must get a release and the new buyer does not receive any credits.

Own the property for 15 years

Remember you are getting these tax credits for ten years. That is a lot of savings over a long period of time. However, if you don't want to do everything that is necessary for these credits because you are too busy running your business, you may say "I'm sorry, I would love to have these tax credits, but this game is not for me."

Most small investors do not have the legal expertise and backup to go out and do all the things necessary to qualify a building and tenants. Some big financial companies have divisions of their companies which put together these low income housing credit programs. They may attract 100 people in a limited partnership to invest $15,000 each. $15,000 times 100—gives them $1.5 million to work with. If they leveraged that at 1,000% or ten times this amount, they could purchase 15 million dollars worth of buildings.

Your credit is based on the percentage of ownership you have in the partnership. The general partner of this limited partnership may choose to keep some of the credits. If the general partner keeps 40% of the credits, it would still leave 60% for each limited partner. This means that 60% of the $15 million put up is for the limited partners. Divide this by 100 and each limited partner receives a $6,300 tax credit. You contributed $15,000 of your hard earned money, but you come up with substantial credits— almost as much as the $15,000. Divide the $6,300 by ten years, and you have $630 per year. Hopefully the property is also producing cash flow, growth and tax deduction. This adds a lot of pizazz to our investing.

> YOUR CREDIT IS BASED ON PERCENTAGE OF OWNERSHIP

The last time I was talking about this low income housing to a friend, he said, "You know, I would love to do it, but I just don't have any excess cash around right now." Let me take time out here and address this. Let's say you're making $30,000 to $40,000 a year at the 15 to 28% tax bracket. You're still paying about $6,000 or $7,000. What if you could find a small group investment, like a limited partnership, that needs investors at the $5,000 or $10,000 range? If you say, "I don't have $10,000 dollars to put into the partnership." I'll counter with, "But you are going to dig up $6,000 to $7,000 to pay the IRS. You are going to write out a check no matter what." Call it a payroll deduction, call it whatever, you are still paying the IRS money. What would happen if instead of writing the IRS a check for $6,000 or $7,000 dollars, you would write a $5,000 to $10,000 dollar check to this Limited Partnership and become one of the unit holders? Then when it comes time to pay your taxes, you don't have to pay that $6,000 to $7,000 dollars because you received the credits produced by the partnership's building to offset any taxes you owe.

These two opportunities can enable you to zero out: deductions from rental real estate against your active income and show you how you can use low income housing credits.

The good news about these low income housing credits is that they have made these tax credits retroactive to July 1st of 1992. For all buildings qualified at or up to that point in time, this low income housing credit program is available on a permanent basis. That's the good news. Before, they would only make it available for one, two, or three years. Because of this permanency, you are going to see more and more of these Limited Partnerships getting really good at this program to allow investors to offset taxes. This permanent feature is going to bring a lot of power and strength to the real estate industry.

LOW INCOME HOUSING CREDITS MADE RETROACTIVE TO JULY 1992

BUYING OR SELLING A BUSINESS

The next thing I would like to cover is for those of you buying a business or selling an existing business. Let's say you have a company you figure is worth a couple of million dollars or you want to buy a company worth several hundred thousand dollars. If you are going to buy a company, it has to be making as much money or have as many tangible assets as the company itself is worth. Typically when you go to figure out the value of a company, you take the cash flow and multiply it by some number (100 to 300% depending on the "jazz" of the company). A publicly traded company could easily be ten to twenty times the cash flow. For example, if you have cash flow of $400,000 dollars in a business, if traded publicly, that company could easily be worth $4 million. This means that investors are willing to pay $4 million to get into a company that has cash flow of $400,000 dollars (which is a 10 percent return on their money).

Let's talk about a private corporation. This corporation has several things in it: equipment, inventory, employees, mail list, a customer base, and a cash flow. Up until now, if you were to buy this company for $2 million and even if you financed it, you would only be able to deduct certain things—such as the hard tangible assets. There has been a fight brewing for many years with the IRS over this because people who buy businesses would, for example, try to depreciate copyrights they were purchasing with the business which had some value—but they couldn't. In a $2 million purchase they may be able to only deduct $500,000. When I say deduct, I mean deducting by depreciating $500,000 over a five or 10 year period of time and that $500,000 is the equipment, computers, copy machines, et cetera. They could not deduct the intangibles. Therefore they would have to pay tax on the extra $1.5 million of the $2 million.

Under the new tax law, effective as of August 10, 1993, you may now deduct different items that before have been considered intangible, including customized existing software, patents, and copyrights. Other deductible intangibles include a work force in place, the customer list and the

YOU CAN DEDUCT ITEMS ONCE CONSIDERED INTANGIBLE

value of the ongoing concern (what we used to call blue sky). So of the $2 million purchase price, virtually all of it can be deducted now, and amortized over a period of time. Let's look at it from several different perspectives. If you are trying to sell your business for $2 million, and someone is going to pay $500,000 down and $300,000 a year for the next six or seven years at a certain interest rate, that person or company purchasing the business can deduct a lot of these things as an expense at the end of the year. So instead of depreciating the $500,000, they are depreciating the whole $2 million in ten years. That deduction (in a 25 to 35% percent tax bracket) is about $100,000 dollars of the amount they need at the end of the year. So they are able to come up with the money they owe you in large part based on the deduction that they get for being able to depreciate this whole business. This is pretty exciting.

Now let's look at it from the other point of view. If you are trying to buy a business (and now you can deduct all of these intangible things you could not deduct before), you can literally use your future tax savings you are going to make by owning this business to help pay for the business in the future. What does this mean? It means if you are trying to sell your business, you can now sell it for more money. And just knowing what I am showing you here is going to help your CPA put a lot higher value on the business enterprise. So whether you are buying or selling, this is a great way to make sure you're maximizing your tax write offs. Again, this is a new tax law, and it is another exciting thing you can do to make more and save more.

NOW, DEDUCT INTANGIBLES

SUMMARY

I hope that this information is helpful to you. The saddest thing I have to say to you in ending this section is I now have to turn you over to your tax professionals, and most of them don't have complete knowledge in these areas. So I encourage you to get down to your book store and purchase every book that you can on every tax item. The biggest single outlay that most small businesses have is their tax outlay, more than their food, rent, or anything else. We work until May or June of every year, just to pay Uncle Sam. Between him and the state, we are paying a phenomenal amount of money. You can slow it down, but you'll never stop the American Enterprise—it will always find a way to break out and succeed.

So why not learn and study everything we can to save money in this one crucial area? Then learn how to keep your money at home working for you. Let's not send excess money back to Washington, D.C. when we don't have to. Let's keep the money beautifying neighborhoods, creating jobs, and prospering in this economy. Let's put something back into this economy that was not there before. This is America at work and this is your chance to step up to the plate and make a big difference in your life.

> LEARN AND KEEP LEARNING

This is great information, but it will be "greater" if you use it. Most tax professionals do not understand corporate structuring or how to sock aside money in a Pension Plan; they don't understand the great ways you have of making and preserving your wealth. Don't let them shoot down these great ideas. You've got to take the bull by the horns; you've got to go out and make a difference.

CHAPTER FOUR

BIG AND SMALL TAX SAVINGS

A Little History for Fun

Year	Maximum Individual Rate
1914	7%
1916	15%
1917	67%
1918	77%
1920	65%
1921	50%
1924	40%
1926	25%
1934	63%
1936	79%
1941	81%
1942	88%
1944	94%
1945	91%
1951	92%
1954	91%
1964	77%
1970	70%
1981	50%
1987	38.5%
1988	28/33%
1989	28/33%
1990	28/33%
1991	31%
1992	31%
1993	36/39.6%

This next section includes many independent items you can use from time to time. Neither this section, nor this book, is designed to be a comprehensive list of every tax deduction or situation. There are plenty of books like that available in book stores. This section will highlight major strategies which will have a big impact on structuring and the taxes you pay.

NET OPERATING LOSS

In its simplest form, a Net Operating Loss (NOL) is an excess of deductions (expenses) over income. I know that anyone reading this and thinking of their own business, whether it's a sole proprietorship or corporation, would like to seriously eliminate even the thought of their business losing money. But if it does happen, is there any consolation? Yes, there is a possible way of recovering back taxes or not paying substantial amounts of income tax in the future.

AN NOL CAN AFFECT 23 DIFFERENT TAX YEARS

You may also qualify for Net Operating Loss treatment as an individual if you have large casualty losses or have been the victim of theft. We won't deal with individual NOLs here. This is about business.

An NOL may affect 23 different tax years. Obviously it would have to be quite large to do that. The first year affected is the current year.

1) If you're a sole proprietor or a partner in a partnership or have ownership in an "S" Corporation, these losses show up on your individual tax returns.

2) The losses from a partnership or "S" Corporation flow through to you individually on a prorated basis.

3) Regular corporations ("C") take the losses in and of themselves. To a large degree the rules are the same as for individuals.

The second block of years affected by an NOL are the past two. If you are currently experiencing difficulties but have made good money for the past two years, this could be a nice way to recover taxes you paid during that time.

Generally, you must go back to the second past year. IRS Form 1045 will walk you through the process. Your current losses will be deducted from your income back then and a new tax recalculated. This return is also the application for a refund. If you eliminate all that income, you apply any excess losses to the immediate past year. The third block of years is the next twenty years. That's right, a loss this year could eliminate income (and therefore taxes) up to twenty years from now. These losses just wait for income (profit) to be figured and then pounce on them as they come up.

> **CAN ELECT TO USE LOSSES IN THE FUTURE**

IMMEDIATE REFUND

Usually you would apply these losses to past years first. Why? So you can get an immediate refund. Depending on your situation, this could be quite large. However, you don't have to go back; you may use these losses in the future. If you make this election, you cannot change your mind.

Why would you choose such an election? If you have not made that much money in the past three years, but you ascertain that even though this year has been a loser, you expect to make a lot of money in the next few years, it would be well to use these losses to offset that income.

Also, as the tax brackets are rising to horrendous levels, these losses will have a greater impact. For example, if going back with a $10,000 loss, it would reduce business income from $38,000 to $28,000 and you'd get back $1,500 (15% tax rate for a corporation). However, that same loss applied to $108,000 back to $98,000 saves you about $3,400. And that's cash in your pocket.

GO FIGURE

You may have an NOL if your income is less than your expenses. It's simple, right? Well, not quite. Now you must make adjustments and eliminate certain deductions completely to see if you have a real NOL.

I want to cover the individual first because it is the most extensive and complicated. Filling out Form 1045 (Schedule A) will be easier if we define a few terms:

1) Business Deductions

These encompass all normal business deductions and the following:

   a) Personal theft losses

   b) Moving expenses to a new job

   c) Casualty losses

   d) State tax on business income

   e) Rental real estate losses

   f) If you are on the accrual method of accounting, losses from the sale of accounts receivable

   g) Part of employee business expense—travel, work clothes, union dues

   h) Losses on sale of 1244 stock, but only up to that amount which qualifies as an ordinary loss

2) Non-Business Deductions

This list is not quite so long:

   a) Medical expenses

   b) Alimony

   c) Contributions to charities

   d) Contribution to IRAs or a Keogh plan

3) Business Income

This includes the following:

   a) Income from your business or trade

b) Any salary you receive

c) Your income from partnership or "S" Corporation

d) Gain from sale of real estate (used in business)

e) Rental Income

4) Non-Business Income

This type of income includes:

a) Dividends

b) Annuities

c) Interest on investments

There are a few limitations on the deductions you may take:

1) To be deductible, your capital losses can't exceed capital gains.

2) Non-business deductions can't be deducted if they exceed non-business income added to non-business capital gains remaining after you deduct non-business capital losses.

3) However, you can deduct business capital losses but only to the extent that business capital gains and non-business capital gains are offset by non-business capital losses and non-business deductions.

Those last two are quite a mouthful. See why you need a good tax preparation specialist?

[Note: these losses, once applied to past income, adjust the income downward. This will have an affect on other calculations based on AGI (adjusted gross income) such as medical deductions.]

CORPORATIONS

Corporations are much simpler. A corporation does not have all these different adjustments. It simply calculates the NOL by subtracting deductions from income.

One note of caution: in a different section I mentioned the 70% exclusion rule wherein a corporation may ignore, as income, 70% of dividend income received from other corporations. In calculating an NOL, this exclusion won't apply.

CORPORATIONS ARE SIMPLER THAN SOLE PROPRIETORSHIPS

If you anticipate losing money in your corporation this year, you may extend the time to pay last year's (immediate preceding year's) income tax. Follow the instructions on Form 1138 to accomplish this.

FORMS

As mentioned before, an individual may file Form 1045, Application for Tentative Refund. This form must be filed within one year of the actual NOL year. The IRS takes up to three months to act on the refund.

Form 1040X, Amended US Individual Income Tax Return, gives you up to three years to file. Corporations should use Form 1139, Corporation Application for Tentative Refund. This should be filed within one year of your NOL year. It would be preferable to file it with the tax return for that year. Also, like the 1040X the corporation may file an 1120X up to three years after the NOL year.

USE THE RIGHT FORM

HOW TO AVOID AUDITS

There is no need here to belabor how to avoid an audit. Every book store in the country has several books on taxation (many written wholly or partially by former Internal Revenue agents), and most of these books contain a lot of information on avoiding or dealing with audits. It has not been the purpose of this book to give tired, worn out information which you can find elsewhere, but I will give a few basic strategies. The thrust of this whole book has been to educate you about the many possibilities in structuring your affairs to minimize taxes (both federal and state), and eliminate risk and unnecessary exposure (bypass the probate process, et cetera). If these legal entities are properly established, they will be your greatest safeguard against intrusion. Here are some helpful points:

1) Avoid having your entities all look the same—same type of entity, same directors, same shareholders with the same percentages of ownership.

2) Have different enterprises with different addresses.

3) Never send in your returns in the same envelope or at the same time.

> AVOID HAVING YOUR ENTITIES LOOK THE SAME

4) Treat them as completely different entities and have each of them treat you (i.e., your contract for work, your compensation, your responsibilities, et cetera) separately.

5) Structure your accounting systems to have the end product conform to the IRS form you will submit.

6) When possible (especially easy for individual), use the name and address label the IRS sends on its packet of forms.

7) If you receive 1099 Forms, either individually, or as a company, check out the details and verify for accuracy.

8) Use ALL of the forms required by the IRS. Just deducting an item or including some number may cause an extra look, even if the item is allowable.

9) Verify that your $2,000 IRA contribution is deductible. Yes, you can contribute $2,000 per working spouse or $2,250 if only one spouse is working and yes, the contribution can have earnings for your future retirement, but no, it may not be a deductible item. If

you or your spouse actively participate in a plan at work, then you may not deduct your contribution if you make more than $35,000 as a single person, or $50,000 married.

10) If you have fluctuating income, take care to avoid paying excess estimated taxes. The IRS calculates income as if it were the same every quarter. If you have extra (large) income one quarter, their calculations may have you paying too much in subsequent quarters. Fill out Form 2210 which shows your computations.

11) Make sure you report items on the proper line. If something is entered improperly, the IRS treats it as if it didn't happen.

12) Examine the records that verify charitable contributions. Provide the necessary information to back up your donations, i.e., receipts or a statement acknowledging your donation. You can list a description of each item. The new rules make it mandatory to list and have documentation for all gifts over $250.

13) If you use a tax preparer, get your information to him/her as early as possible. Also, try to "get on the front burner" by getting a completion date. If not you may get shuffled while they take care of the "squeaky wheels."

14) Sign your return.

In short, common sense will keep you out of trouble.

YEAR END TAX MANEUVERING

USE COMMON SENSE

There are some effective tactics you can take regarding April 15th, tax day. Because situations are so varied, I encourage you to work with your CPA, not on April 14th, but sometime in October, November or at the latest, December to see if there is anything you could and should be doing to mini-mize your taxes for that year or to spread out the year's taxes into other years.

1) If you do have a company that loses money, make sure you review the NOL section for maximizing your write offs not only this year but also in other years.

YOU CAN MINIMIZE YOUR TAXES

2) If you do take any kind of compensation from stock options, you may want to choose which year you want to use those options.

3) If you're selling properties, you may want to consider the installment sales method for spreading out the capital gains over a period of time.

4) You may want to prepay your property taxes for the previous year or the next year.

5) Technically, interest that you pay is claimed or deducted in the year that it's paid. You are probably well aware that your January 1st house payment is interest for the month of December. But because the payment is made in January, it's a deduction for the following year. However, if you were to make your January 1st payment on December 31st, you would be able to deduct that interest in this current year.

6) Charitable Contributions. If you have appre-ciated value in some of your assets, such as stocks, you may want to give those to a char-ity to avoid capital gains. This would help the charity and also give you tax deductions at the end of the year.

7) If you have not established a KEOGH plan or a corporate pension plan, you must do so

by the end of the year. However, you have until April 15th or longer (with extensions) to make contributions into the plan.

8) If you are an employee and participate in a 401(k) plan or any other type of tax quali- fied retirement plan, you may make contri- butions clear up to April 15th.

9) You may want to pay many of your expenses early, or if you think you're going to have a larger income the next year, delay for a few days paying those (before the end of the year) so the payment of those expenses goes into the next calendar year.

AFTER YEAR END (POST DECEMBER 31ST)

OPPORTUNITIES

1) Contributing to your business retirement account, even up to April 15th (or longer with extensions) will reduce your AGI. Many other calculations (casualty losses, medical) are based on a percentage of AGI and reducing your AGI may increase your deductions.

CONTRIBUTE TO YOUR RETIREMENT ACCOUNT UP TO APRIL 15TH

2) If you are self-employed and did not open a KEOGH plan by December 31st of the previous year, you can still start up a SEP-IRA and possibly put in an amount larger than $2,000 into a regular IRA.

3) IRAs. Even if you participate in a com- pany pension plan, you can still put $2,000 into your own IRA. Whether it's currently deductible or not depends on your income level. See your tax advisor.

4) Extensions. You can't avoid paying taxes with an extension (you must estimate your tax and send it in) but you can extend your filing time four months to August 15. Use IRS Form 4868.

5) Payment Extension. If payment of your taxes would create a hardship, you can request an extension for payment by using IRS Form 1127.

6) Check information on 1099s and other information statements for accuracy. Ask for a revised one if there is an error.

7) Retirement Plan Payouts. If you took a distribution from your retirement plan, even an IRA rollover, make sure you record the payout and rollover in the income section. If you don't, the IRS may pull your return for inquiry. They may assume you just spent the money and did not roll it to another IRA.

The new tax law is so complicated that it will take an expert tax preparer to help you understand your tax liability and the differences in calculating it, especially if you're a high income earner and have to deal with the alternative minimum tax. However, there are some valuable techniques you can use to minimize the tax bite.

1) Delay income, especially bonuses. *[Note: if you think your rates may be lower (but deductions fewer) next year—maybe an early bonus would be better.]*

2) Pay expenses early to get them into this tax year. Hopefully, you're using a fiscal year-end, so don't calculate everything based on December 31st.

3) If available, take compensation in stock options and delay exercising them until later.

4) Borrow money from your corporation so you don't have taxable income (See "Forgivable Loans").

5) Prepay state and property taxes.

6) Use an installment sale or delay the closing on the sale of real estate property.

7) If, after the first of the year, after recalculating your company profits or your income, you find it is higher, place more into your 401(k), KEOGH, Corporate pension, SEP-IRA, or regular IRA.

8) Don't wait until the end of the year, or even April 15th of the next year, to put money into your retirement accounts. Get the tax deferred-growth aspect of these accounts working for you as early as possible.

9) If you haven't established a pension account, do so by your year-end or your corporate year-end. You have until April 15th to fund it, or longer with extensions. (Corporations with off year-ends have other dates.)

10) Make charitable contributions with appreciated stocks, real estate, et cetera. You may not get the deduction on the full value, but you won't have to pay capital gain taxes. In most instances, if an appreciated asset is donated directly, it's fully deductible.

Tax filing is turning into a balancing act. You'll need experienced and wise counsel to calculate your best moves. With the added advantage of entity planning as explained throughout this book, you should be able to reduce your tax liability 15 to 30% and sometimes to zero.

REDUCE YOUR TAX LIABILITY 15 TO 30%.

TAX POINTS

1) Part of the withholding tax is for Medicare (1.45% if employee, matched by the employer, and 2.90% if self-employed). It ended at certain income levels at one time, but that is no longer the case. While FICA still ends at $62,700

(1996), the Medicare tax is now stretched to infinity, which is another reason to try to avoid earned income.

2) After reaching $172,050 of AGI if married and $114,700 if single, we lose 2% of our personal exemptions.

3) Capital gains taxes are limited to 20% (or 10% in certain circumstances.)

SOCIAL SECURITY TAX IS BASED ON THE FIRST **$62,700**

4) Meals and entertainment expenses are severely limited. However, if you hold a marketing meeting for your sales staff to improve your business, it's fully deductible.

5) It's relatively easy to get a Federal ID number for your corporation, trust, or partnership. Look over the SS-4 and be ready with the answer. Call the regional processing center and within five minutes you'll have the number. If you don't have the SS-4 in front of you, they won't process it then—you'll have to call back. Also, you'll still have to mail in or fax the signed form. This is advantageous if you need the number now instead of in a few weeks, say for opening a bank account.

6) If you invest in mutual funds and reinvest the income, you don't have to claim it as income. It adjusts the basis and you'll be taxed when you sell.

7) If you cash in early on CDs, the early withdrawal penalties are deductible.

8) Safe deposit box fees are deductible if used for business or for holding tax documents.

9) IRA trustee fees are deductible. One hint: pay with a separate check, don't let them just deduct the fee from your account.

10) Local personal property taxes are deductible if they are based on the value of the property,

such as a car. States included are Arizona, California, Colorado, Georgia, Indiana, Iowa, Maine, Massachusetts, Minnesota, Michigan, Missouri, Nebraska, New Hampshire, Oklahoma, Washington and Wyoming.

11) Job hunting fees are deductible, including reasonable expenses for meals and entertainment.

STATES WHERE

PERSONAL PROPERTY

TAXES ARE DEDUCTIBLE

12) If you have more than one employer, they all may be deducting Social Security taxes.

13) Charitable giving of assets held over a year are deducted at the full value.

14) The cost of setting up and fees for operating a Pension Plan are deductible expenses and should be paid by the plan sponsor—maybe your corporation.

15) Parents are responsible to file for children if they have $4,150 of earned income, but no unearned income, or a combination of $650 of earned income and unearned income. Gifts don't count.

16) Life insurance trust. Owning your policy will make sure the life insurance proceeds do not show up in your taxable estate.

17) It's a good idea to check all information received on your 1099s or W-2. There are often mistakes. Ask for a new (revised) one if you find mistakes.

18) If you are supporting dependent parents (even if they don't live with you) you can claim them as an exemption. Use IRS Form 2120. If multiple people are paying (your brothers and sisters) and you provide over half, you still get the exemption.

Installment Sales

If you have owned an asset and sell that asset, wherein you are going to receive some of the profits in more than one taxable year, then that sale will probably qualify as an installment sale. The IRS form you are going to use for calculating the taxes you owe is Internal Revenue Code Form 6252.

Many of you have probably heard about the way I do real estate deals—buy and sell rapidly, on contract, get your cash back and get on to other deals, but leave behind a deed of trust recorded against the property with income coming in over a long period of time. While doing deals, it became very important to be able to claim the profit over a period of time and not have to claim all the profit in the year of sale. Obviously, I did not receive all this profit in the year of sale and if I was going to receive it over a period of time, I wanted to be able to claim the income over that same period.

> RECEIVE PROFIT OVER A PERIOD OF TIME

For example, I bought a property for $80,000 and we sold it for $100,000. In selling it, we took a $5,000 down payment, carried back a $95,000 contract and wrapped around the existing loan of $80,000. We would have a capital gain of $20,000. This is a difference between the $80,000 basis in the property and the $100,000 sale price. I am not receiving anywhere close to that $20,000 in the year of sale. I am going to receive the money over a period of time. How and in what format? The $100,000 I am going to receive is partly made up of the down payment ($5,000) and then $95,000 coming in monthly payments.

Let's say the monthly payments are $950. For the sake of this example, $50 of the $950 is principal and $900 is interest (obviously this amount changes every month, but we are going to leave it the same just for this example).

How are we going to claim our $20,000 profit? When I ask this in the seminars, everyone says, "You've got $5,000 right now"—but that's not true. Part of the $100,000 we're receiving is our original base or cost of the property—in this example, $80,000. The other part, $20,000, is the actual capital gain in selling this property. If I were to claim all of the $50 principal payments over a period of time, that full amount added to the down payment amount of $5,000 would equal $100,000.

Spreading out this whole amount of money over a period of time is going to save us a lot of money. The amount of money I claim is still not based on the $100,000, but on the $20,000. Part of the $100,000, again, is the $20,000 capital gain. I need to know what part of each installment that comes in on the $100,000 represents the $20,000. Remember, the other part will be the basis in the property.

The way to calculate this is to take the profit or gain and divide it by the selling price of the property. In this example— look at the figure below—you'll see it equals the installment sales ratio. I would take $20,000, divide it by $100,000 and get .2 or 20%. This is the amount I'll have to claim of every principal payment I have received (including the down payment which is truly a principal payment).

Let's get more specific by continuing this example and see how it pans out for this year. For the sake of simplicity, let's say I made this deal in January. So I have twelve of these $50 checks coming in which would equal $600, I take that $600 plus the $5,000 down payment I received, totaling $5,600. That is the principal payment I have received. Now I have to claim 20% of that or $1,120 (that's what I will have to claim this year). Why is it so big this year? Simply because I received a large down payment. Will I receive a down payment next year? Probably not. Sometimes there are down payments split up over a number years, but in our example there is a one time down payment of $5,000. Next year, I'll have to claim the amount of the principal I receive next year.

Let's say by this time the $50 grows to an average of $60 a month. Sixty dollars a month of principal received for 12 months is $720. That is what I received, so I will have to claim 20% of that, or $144. Add that $144 to the $1,120 and what we're going to take in next year and the year after that and eventually all those little amounts of money will add up to the $20,000. I will be able to claim the $20,000 profit over the course of the loan which could be 25 or 30 years down the road.

Go back up and look at the 20%. It came out even with a zero because all of our numbers were even. If we changed even one of these numbers by $5 or $10, you could see this could be a decimal which would go on forever. The IRS suggests you use five or six decimal points. I believe, in this case, we should do one better than the IRS requests of us. Go out at least six or seven decimal points. If I'm shooting a gun at an object 200 yards away, to move the barrel of the gun even an eighth of an inch (even though it's a small amount of movement) the results at the other end will be quite substantial. If you go out six or seven decimal points, you'll be within a fraction of the amount you should have claimed over the course of the 25 to 30 years.

Back to our example. As I mentioned before, the IRS form you'll use for calculating this is Form 6252. In this example, I have not had any cost of improvements. If this has been rental property, where depreciation is allowed over a period of time, I would probably have cost of improvements. I have also not added in any expenses of sale. I did this for simplicity sake. On Form 6252 you can see if I had this as a depreciation, on part 1, line 7 or 8, I would deduct out the depreciation I had taken and that is where I would calculate a new basis on the property.

Likewise, if I sold the property and had many expenses of sale, that would be calculated and would lessen the profits. The installment sales ratio would be a lesser amount, therefore I could claim less over a long period of time. This is not just for real property. It could be for buying and selling refrigerators, if you did it incidental to another business. It could be for anything you are selling; but most people do not sell a lot of other things on an installment sales basis—the most typical being real estate.

USE FORM 6252

However, another big area where this could be used would be in the selling of a business. Many businesses are sold on some kind of an installment payment. People either pay part of the money now and the balance of the money within a year or two, or they pay a deposit now and pay off the equity over a period of time.

For instance, if you had a bicycle shop worth $100,000 and you sold it by taking $25,000 in a carry-back note for $75,000—you could claim the balance of the profits over a period of time. Let's say with the bicycle shop you sold for $100,000, you had a $20,000 basis. That is what you spent to start the business. Now you have an $80,000 gain in this business. If you run the numbers again, you'd have $80,000 divided by $100,000 and your installment sales ratio would be 80%. Let's say you've already depreciated out your start-up cost. Let's get even more specific by saying that your basis is zero. Your profit would be $100,000; you would divide it by the selling price ($100,000) and you would have 100%.

Therefore, you get to spread out claiming your profits over a period of time. If you get a $25,000 deposit for selling it, you would have to claim 100% of that $25,000 this year. The person is paying you $2,000 a month at a certain interest rate over a period of time. You would obviously have to claim the interest income on the money received as interest income. You make a profit and claim that profit as income. Part of the monthly payment represents the gain—do you have to claim that? The answer is, "Yes." You take the principal you receive, times your installment sales ratio, which in this example would be 100%. Therefore, the point is, you get to spread out claiming your profits over a long period of time.

So, you have income that you are having to claim as income, but you get to claim it as you receive it. One of the things you want to avoid is phantom income, which is income from zero coupon bonds, "S" Corporations or Limited Partnerships that you actually do not receive but are still responsible for the tax liabilities.

SECTION 179 INTERNAL REVENUE CODE

Section 179 deals with the amount businesses can immediately deduct on equipment purchases. Sometimes Section 179 is referred to as "asset expensing." Let's discuss equipment purchases and how they are handled in a normal business sense. If you buy equipment for business purposes, that

AVOID PHANTOM INCOME

equipment is usually deducted and depreciated over a five-year period of time. For example, if you were to purchase $8,000 worth of equipment for your business, you would divide $8,000 by five and take $1,600 a year in deductions. On your Schedule C, if you are sole proprietor, or on your Form 1120, if you are a corporation, where it says depreciation expense, you would deduct this $1,600. If you are in a 15% tax bracket you would save 15% of $1,600. If you are in a 25, 28, or 31% tax bracket, by calculating in the different entities, that is how much your actual savings would be. I think equipment purchases should be able to be deductible right now because many kinds of equipment are obsolete by the time you buy them at the store and get them back to your office. Some equipment is deducted on the three-year property basis, but most is deducted on a five-year basis. How would you like to be able to take the full amount of the equipment purchased and deduct all of it right now? Examine the following types of equipment.

1) Have you purchased office equipment, i.e., copy machines, typewriters, or any other kinds of desk and office equipment?

2) Have you purchased a computer or any other kind of computer related equipment?

3) Have you purchased any kind of phone equipment, fax machines, mobile phones, car phones, or any other kinds of phone systems for your office?

4) Have you purchased a car or truck for your business? (If you do not have a car or truck for your business, you can do so, and if you are in business or getting ready to start up a business, some percentages of your car or truck can be allocated to business expense.

5) Have you purchased any other kind of special equipment for any other kind of unique businesses?

If you have answered "yes" to any of these questions, then you qualify for Section 179. Here's how it works. You purchase equipment with any kind of financing—something down and the balance due over a period of time, some kind of lease arrangements with the purchase option at the end or 100% financing. The arrangements you use do not matter. You may now take up to $18,000 of equipment purchases in 1997 (increasing gradually to $25,000), under any financing format and immediately expense that in the year of purchase. For example, if you have a business making $50,000 a year and you purchased $8,000 worth of equipment (this could be made up of several different pieces of equipment) you may now immediately deduct it off the $50,000 this

DEDUCT ALL EQUIPMENT NOW

year. So, instead of making $50,000, your company has a net profit of $42,000. You are going to pay, if it is a corporation, 15% less taxes on the $8,000. If you are a sole proprietorship, in that range—you'll be paying 28% taxes, so you'll save 28% of the $8,000—which is almost $2,500 cash in your pocket. Do not send it to the IRS. Keep the money and spend it on movies, groceries, whatever!

The form you need to use is Form 4562. On this form you list the different types of equipment, some identification numbers, and the amount that you paid for them. In our example they add up to $8,000. So you would take the $8,000 and transfer it from Form 4562 over to your Schedule C. It would go on line 13, on Schedule C, as another deduction. Where your business was previously making $50,000, by subtracting this extra $8,000 in deductions your business has a net profit of $42,000. That net profit transfers over to your 1040 and you have $42,000 of income on line 13 compared to $50,000. The point is quite obvious, you are now paying substantially less in income taxes. By the way, the higher your tax bracket, the more impact this has on your tax situation. Do you remember that dreaded Social Security Tax—the 15% plus payments we have to make for FICA tax purposes? When you transfer from your Schedule C, it says the profits on the Schedule C are entered on your Form 1040 and Schedule SE. Rather than writing the $50,000 amount on your SE, you now enter $42,000. So now, you are not only saving money on Federal income taxes, but you are also saving money on Federal Social Security taxes. Another big savings, especially at the 15.3% rate.

HOW TO USE FORM 4562

CASH IN YOUR POCKET

For some of you there can even be a triple whammy. If you live in a state that has income tax, most states follow federal guidelines. You can check with your local CPA to see if yours does. Most states allow Section

179-type deductions. You now have savings on Federal Income Taxes, Federal Social Security Taxes and on State Income Taxes. This is one of the simplest tax deductions—just by purchasing equipment from other small businesses. Under the old tax law it was $10,000 rather than $18,000.

There are other implications from this part of the tax code. Let's say, for example, you purchased $22,000 worth of equipment. You could take the first $18,000 and deduct it right now, but what do you do with that other $4,000—the difference between the $22,000 and $18,000? You take the $18,000 up front "bonus type" deduction right now and the balance of the $4,000 is depreciated over the remaining seven years of the seven year depreciation schedule. Next year you are also allowed to buy more equipment up to the $18,000. This is $18,000 each and every year.

$18,000 EACH AND EVERY YEAR

Automobiles can only be a small percentage of the $18,000. It would be better for you to depreciate the car under its regular depreciation basis. Most cars and light trucks can be depreciated in five years and that schedule is usually higher than what is allowed in Section 179. So you can deduct the car in five years and you can still have $18,000 worth of other equipment.

Section 179 cannot cause a loss. Let's say you have started up a small business and you net $15,000. You have, in fact, purchased $18,000 worth of equipment. You cannot go to a negative $3,000. However, Section 179 can take you down to zero. It cannot put you into a loss position. What do you do with the other $3,000 that you could not use? It can immediately be used the next year as part of the $18,000. You would only have to come up with $15,000 more worth of equipment to totally max out the $18,000 the very next year.

SECTION 179 CANNOT CAUSE A LOSS

Most types of investments are prorated by the month when computing taxes. The best time of the year to buy rental real estate, for example, is in January. In January you get $^{12}/_{12}$ of the first year write offs. In February you get $^{11}/_{12}$ and in March $^{10}/_{12}$ and so on. However, Section 179 is not prorated by the month. This simply means you could buy equipment in December and get the tax write offs as if you bought the equipment in January. What this really means is you could go out between Christmas and New Years, buy a bunch of equipment, finance it 100%, haul it back over to your office and get a $18,000 deduction on the very last day of the year.

EXAMPLE A

In the first example we will depreciate $18,000 of equipment purchased with a seven year schedule. You'll notice $3,000 on Schedule C, line 13. The savings are minimal and depend on your tax bracket because ultimately this will end up on your Form 1040.

If you follow our example, you'll see the net profit of $92,366 includes the deduction of $3,000. If you're married, filing jointly (in this range) you'll save 28% of $3,000 or $840. But look at Example B and the accompanying Form 4562.

EXAMPLE B

This time we will use Form 4562 to take the full deductions. Remember, this is called "asset expensing." We are also making the assumption you only purchased $18,000 worth of equipment. If less than $18,000, you can take the entire amount. If over $18,000, depreciate the balance.

[Note: if you do not get to the full $18,000 and you purchase a car or light truck for business, you may want to "SEC 179" that purchase. However, cars and light trucks are depreciated in five years anyway. Maybe you should elect to depreciate them on a regular schedule.]

Here you have a net profit of $77,366. Your savings (assuming this is your only income) is 28% of $18,000 which equals $5,040. It really is better than this because:

1) You've lowered your FICA tax.

2) Many states allow Section 179 deductions so you save on your state income tax.

3) Corporations also qualify for Section 179.

EXAMPLE A

SCHEDULE C (Form 1040) Department of the Treasury Internal Revenue Service (O)	**Profit or Loss From Business** (Sole Proprietorship) ▶ Partnerships, joint ventures, etc., must file Form 1065. ▶ Attach to Form 1040 or Form 1041. ▶ See Instructions for Schedule C (Form 1040).	OMB No. 1545-0074 19 Attachment Sequence No. 09

Name of proprietor	Social security number (SSN)
Adam Jones	

A	Principal business or profession, including product or service (see page C-1)	B	Enter principal business code (see page C-6) ▶

C	Business name. If no separate business name, leave blank. ABC Consulting Services	D	Employer ID number (EIN), if any

E Business address (including suite or room no.) ▶ ....
  City, town or post office, state, and ZIP code

F Accounting method: **(1)** ☐ Cash **(2)** ☐ Accrual **(3)** ☐ Other (specify) ▶ ....

G Did you "materially participate" in the operation of this business during 19   ? If "No," see page C-2 for limit on losses. ☐ Yes ☐ No

H If you started or acquired this business during 19   , check here . . . . ▶ ☐

Part I Income

1	Gross receipts or sales. **Caution:** If this income was reported to you on Form W-2 and the "Statutory employee" box on that form was checked, see page C-2 and check here . . . . ▶ ☐	1	214,891
2	Returns and allowances	2	2,200
3	Subtract line 2 from line 1	3	212,691
4	Cost of goods sold (from line 42 on page 2)	4	42,130
5	**Gross profit.** Subtract line 4 from line 3	5	170,561
6	Other income, including Federal and state gasoline or fuel tax credit or refund (see page C-2) . . .	6	
7	**Gross income.** Add lines 5 and 6 . . . . ▶	7	170,561

Part II Expenses. Enter expenses for business use of your home **only** on line 30.

8	Advertising	8	3,940	19	Pension and profit-sharing plans	19	15,200
9	Bad debts from sales or services (see page C-3) . .	9		20	Rent or lease (see page C-4): a Vehicles, machinery, and equipment .	20a	
10	Car and truck expenses (see page C-3)	10	2,185	b Other business property . .	20b	
11	Commissions and fees . .	11	1,580	21	Repairs and maintenance . .	21	750
12	Depletion	12		22	Supplies (not included in Part III) .	22	1,200
13	Depreciation and section 179 expense deduction (not included in Part III) (see page C-3) . .	13	3,000	23	Taxes and licenses	23	850
				24	Travel, meals, and entertainment:		
14	Employee benefit programs (other than on line 19) . . .	14		a Travel	24a	2,650
15	Insurance (other than health) .	15	1,952	b Meals and entertainment .	1,850	
16	Interest:			c Enter 50% of line 24b subject to limitations (see page C-4) .	370	
a	Mortgage (paid to banks, etc.) .	16a	2,750	d Subtract line 24c from line 24b .	24d	1,480
b	Other	16b		25	Utilities	25	1,350
17	Legal and professional services	17	2,200	26	Wages (less employment credits) .	26	5,800
18	Office expense	18	6,808	27	Other expenses (from line 48 on page 2)	27	24,500

28	**Total expenses** before expenses for business use of home. Add lines 8 through 27 in columns . ▶	28	78,195
29	Tentative profit (loss). Subtract line 28 from line 7	29	92,366
30	Expenses for business use of your home. Attach Form 8829	30	
31	**Net profit or (loss).** Subtract line 30 from line 29. • If a profit, enter on **Form 1040, line 12,** and ALSO on **Schedule SE, line 2** (statutory employees, see page C-5). Estates and trusts, enter on Form 1041, line 3. • If a loss, you MUST go on to line 32.	31	92,366
32	If you have a loss, check the box that describes your investment in this activity (see page C-5). • If you checked 32a, enter the loss on **Form 1040, line 12,** and ALSO on **Schedule SE, line 2** (statutory employees, see page C-5). Estates and trusts, enter on Form 1041, line 3. • If you checked 32b, you MUST attach **Form 6198.**	32a ☐ All investment is at risk. 32b ☐ Some investment is not at risk.

For Paperwork Reduction Act Notice, see Form 1040 instructions.   Cat. No. 11334P   Schedule C (Form 1040)

Schedule C (Form 1040)

Page **2**

Part III   Cost of Goods Sold (see page C-5)

33   Method(s) used to value closing inventory: **a** ☐ Cost   **b** ☐ Lower of cost or market   **c** ☐ Other (attach explanation)

34   Was there any change in determining quantities, costs, or valuations between opening and closing inventory? If "Yes," attach explanation . . . . ☐ Yes   ☐ No

35 Inventory at beginning of year. If different from last year's closing inventory, attach explanation	35	
36 Purchases less cost of items withdrawn for personal use	36	42,130
37 Cost of labor. Do not include salary paid to yourself	37	
38 Materials and supplies	38	
39 Other costs	39	
40 Add lines 35 through 39	40	42,130
41 Inventory at end of year	41	
42 **Cost of goods sold.** Subtract line 41 from line 40. Enter the result here and on page 1, line 4	42	42,130

Part IV   **Information on Your Vehicle.** Complete this part ONLY if you are claiming car or truck expenses on line 10 and are not required to file Form 4562 for this business. See the instructions for line 13 on page C-3 to find out if you must file.

43   When did you place your vehicle in service for business purposes? (month, day, year) ▶ ...../...../.....

44   Of the total number of miles you drove your vehicle during 19 , enter the number of miles you used your vehicle for:

a Business .... **b** Commuting .... **c** Other ....

45   Do you (or your spouse) have another vehicle available for personal use? . . . . ☐ Yes   ☐ No

46   Was your vehicle available for use during off-duty hours? . . . . ☐ Yes   ☐ No

47a   Do you have evidence to support your deduction? . . . . ☐ Yes   ☐ No

b If "Yes," is the evidence written? . . . . ☐ Yes   ☐ No

Part V   **Other Expenses.** List below business expenses not included on lines 8–26 or line 30.

	42,130
48 **Total other expenses.** Enter here and on page 1, line 27	48 42,130

✿ Printed on recycled paper   ° U.S. GOVERNMENT PRINTING OFFICE: 407-199

EXAMPLE B

SCHEDULE C (Form 1040)	**Profit or Loss From Business** (Sole Proprietorship)	OMB No. 1545-0074
Department of the Treasury Internal Revenue Service (O)	▶ Partnerships, joint ventures, etc., must file Form 1065. ▶ Attach to Form 1040 or Form 1041. ▶ See Instructions for Schedule C (Form 1040).	19 Attachment Sequence No. 09

Name of proprietor	Social security number (SSN)
Adam Jones	

A Principal business or profession, including product or service (see page C-1) | **B** Enter principal business code (see page C-6) ▶

C Business name. If no separate business name, leave blank. | **D** Employer ID number (EIN), if any

ABC Consulting Services

E Business address (including suite or room no.) ▶ ....
City, town or post office, state, and ZIP code

F Accounting method: (1) ☐ Cash (2) ☐ Accrual (3) ☐ Other (specify) ▶ ....

G Did you "materially participate" in the operation of this business during 19 ? If "No," see page C-2 for limit on losses. ☐ Yes ☐ No

H If you started or acquired this business during 19 , check here .... ▶ ☐

Part I Income

1	Gross receipts or sales. **Caution:** If this income was reported to you on Form W-2 and the "Statutory employee" box on that form was checked, see page C-2 and check here .... ▶ ☐	1	214,891
2	Returns and allowances	2	2,200
3	Subtract line 2 from line 1	3	212,691
4	Cost of goods sold (from line 42 on page 2)	4	42,130
5	**Gross profit.** Subtract line 4 from line 3	5	170,561
6	Other income, including Federal and state gasoline or fuel tax credit or refund (see page C-2) ...	6	
7	**Gross income.** Add lines 5 and 6 .... ▶	7	170,561

Part II Expenses. Enter expenses for business use of your home **only** on line 30.

8	Advertising	8	3,940	19 Pension and profit-sharing plans	19	15,200
9	Bad debts from sales or services (see page C-3)	9		20 Rent or lease (see page C-4):		
				a Vehicles. machinery, and equipment	20a	
10	Car and truck expenses (see page C-3)	10	2,185	b Other business property	20b	
11	Commissions and fees	11	1,580	21 Repairs and maintenance	21	750
12	Depletion	12		22 Supplies (not included in Part III)	22	1,200
13	Depreciation and section 179 expense deduction (not included in Part III) (see page C-3)	13	18,000	23 Taxes and licenses	23	850
				24 Travel, meals, and entertainment:		
14	Employee benefit programs (other than on line 19)	14		a Travel	24a	2,650
15	Insurance (other than health)	15	1,952	b Meals and entertainment 1,850		
16	Interest:			c Enter 50% of line 24b subject to limitations (see page C-4) 370		
a	Mortgage (paid to banks, etc.)	16a	2,750	d Subtract line 24c from line 24b	24d	1,480
b	Other	16b		25 Utilities	25	1,350
17	Legal and professional services	17	2,200	26 Wages (less employment credits)	26	5,800
18	Office expense	18	6,808	27 Other expenses (from line 48 on page 2)	27	24,500

28	**Total expenses** before expenses for business use of home. Add lines 8 through 27 in columns ▶	28	93,195
29	Tentative profit (loss). Subtract line 28 from line 7	29	77,366
30	Expenses for business use of your home. Attach **Form 8829**	30	
31	**Net profit or (loss).** Subtract line 30 from line 29.		
	• If a profit, enter on **Form 1040, line 12**, and ALSO on **Schedule SE, line 2** (statutory employees, see page C-5). Estates and trusts, enter on Form 1041, line 3.	31	77,366
	• If a loss, you MUST go on to line 32.		
32	If you have a loss, check the box that describes your investment in this activity (see page C-5).		
	• If you checked 32a, enter the loss on **Form 1040, line 12**, and ALSO on **Schedule SE, line 2** (statutory employees, see page C-5). Estates and trusts, enter on Form 1041, line 3.	32a ☐ All investment is at risk. 32b ☐ Some investment is not at risk.	
	• If you checked 32b, you MUST attach **Form 6198.**		

For Paperwork Reduction Act Notice, see Form 1040 instructions.   Cat. No. 11334P   Schedule C (Form 1040)

Schedule C (Form 1040)   Page **2**

Part III   Cost of Goods Sold (see page C-5)

33   Method(s) used to
value closing inventory: **a** ☐ Cost   **b** ☐ Lower of cost or market   **c** ☐ Other (attach explanation)

34   Was there any change in determining quantities, costs, or valuations between opening and closing inventory? If
"Yes," attach explanation . . . . ☐ Yes   ☐ No

35 Inventory at beginning of year. If different from last year's closing inventory, attach explanation . .	**35**	
36 Purchases less cost of items withdrawn for personal use	**36**	
37 Cost of labor. Do not include salary paid to yourself	**37**	
38 Materials and supplies	**38**	
39 Other costs	**39**	
40 Add lines 35 through 39	**40**	
41 Inventory at end of year	**41**	
42 **Cost of goods sold.** Subtract line 41 from line 40. Enter the result here and on page 1, line 4 . .	**42**	

Part IV   **Information on Your Vehicle.** Complete this part **ONLY** if you are claiming car or truck expenses on line 10 and are not required to file Form 4562 for this business. See the instructions for line 13 on page C-3 to find out if you must file.

43   When did you place your vehicle in service for business purposes? (month, day, year) ▶ ..../........./....... .

44   Of the total number of miles you drove your vehicle during 19   , enter the number of miles you used your vehicle for:

  a Business .... **b** Commuting .... **c** Other ....

45   Do you (or your spouse) have another vehicle available for personal use? . . . . ☐ Yes   ☐ No

46   Was your vehicle available for use during off-duty hours?   . . . . ☐ Yes   ☐ No

47a   Do you have evidence to support your deduction?   . . . . ☐ Yes   ☐ No

  b If "Yes," is the evidence written? . . . . ☐ Yes   ☐ No

Part V   **Other Expenses.** List below business expenses not included on lines 8–26 or line 30.

....		
....		
....		
....		
....		
....		
....		
....		
48 **Total other expenses.** Enter here and on page 1, line 27	**48**	

✳ *Printed on recycled paper*   ° U.S. GOVERNMENT PRINTING OFFICE: 407-199

EXAMPLE B (CONTINUED)

Form **4562**	**Depreciation and Amortization**	OMB No. 1545-0172
	(Including Information on Listed Property)	19
Department of the Treasury Internal Revenue Service (O)	▶ See separate instructions. ▶ Attach this form to your return.	Attachment Sequence No. **67**
Name(s) shown on return Adam Jones	Business or activity to which this form relates ABC Consulting Services	Identifying number

Part I   Election To Expense Certain Tangible Property (Section 179) (Note: *If you have any "listed property," complete Part V before you complete Part I.)*

1	Maximum dollar limitation. If an enterprise zone business, see page 2 of the instructions . .	**1**	$18,000
2	Total cost of section 179 property placed in service. See page 2 of the instructions	**2**	18,000
3	Threshold cost of section 179 property before reduction in limitation	**3**	$200,000
4	Reduction in limitation. Subtract line 3 from line 2. If zero or less, enter -0-	**4**	-0-
5	Dollar limitation for tax year. Subtract line 4 from line 1. If zero or less, enter -0-. If married filing separately, see page 2 of the instructions	**5**	18,000

(a) Description of property	**(b)** Cost (business use only)	**(c)** Elected cost	
6 Computer, CD Rom, Printer	10,000	10,000	
Office equipment	8,000	8,000	

7	Listed property. Enter amount from line 27.	**7**	
8	Total elected cost of section 179 property. Add amounts in column (c), lines 6 and 7 . . .	**8**	18,000
9	Tentative deduction. Enter the smaller of line 5 or line 8	**9**	18,000
10	Carryover of disallowed deduction from 19 . See page 2 of the instructions	**10**	-0-
11	Business income limitation. Enter the smaller of business income (not less than zero) or line 5 (see instructions)	**11**	
12	Section 179 expense deduction. Add lines 9 and 10, but do not enter more than line 11 . .	**12**	18,000
13	Carryover of disallowed deduction to 19 . Add lines 9 and 10, less line 12 ▶ **13**		

Note: *Do not use Part II or Part III below for listed property (automobiles, certain other vehicles, cellular telephones, certain computers, or property used for entertainment, recreation, or amusement). Instead, use Part V for listed property.*

Part II   MACRS Depreciation For Assets Placed in Service ONLY During Your 19   Tax Year (Do Not Include Listed Property.)

Section A—General Asset Account Election

14   If you are making the election under section 168(i)(4) to group any assets placed in service during the tax year into one or more general asset accounts, check this box. See page 2 of the instructions . . . . ▶ ☐

Section B—General Depreciation System (GDS) (See page 3 of the instructions.)

(a) Classification of property	**(b)** Month and year placed in service	**(c)** Basis for depreciation (business/investment use only—see instructions)	**(d)** Recovery period	**(e)** Convention	**(f)** Method	**(g)** Depreciation deduction
15a						
b						
c						
d						
e						
f						
g						
h						
i						

NOTE: at press time the new forms were not published. Check with your CPA or local IRS office for the new Form 4562.

Section C—Alternative Depreciation System (ADS) (See page 4 of the instructions.)

16a	Class life				S/L	
b	12-year		12 yrs.		S/L	
c	40-year		40 yrs.	MM	S/L	

Part III   Other Depreciation (Do Not Include Listed Property.) (See page 4 of the instructions.)

17	GDS and ADS deductions for assets placed in service in tax years beginning before 19	**17**	
18	Property subject to section 168(f)(1) election	**18**	
19	ACRS and other depreciation	**19**	

Part IV   Summary (See page 4 of the instructions.)

20	Listed property. Enter amount from line 26.	**20**	
21	**Total.** Add deductions on line 12, lines 15 and 16 in column (g), and lines 17 through 20. Enter here and on the appropriate lines of your return. Partnerships and S corporations—see instructions . .	**21**	
22	For assets shown above and placed in service during the current year, enter the portion of the basis attributable to section 263A costs **22**		

For Paperwork Reduction Act Notice, see page 1 of the separate instructions.   Cat. No. 12906N   Form **4562**

Form 4562

Part V   Listed Property—Automobiles, Certain Other Vehicles, Cellular Telephones, Certain Computers, and Property Used for Entertainment, Recreation, or Amusement

Note: *For any vehicle for which you are using the standard mileage rate or deducting lease expense, complete **only** 23a, 23b, columns (a) through (c) of Section A, all of Section B, and Section C if applicable.*

Section A—Depreciation and Other Information (Caution: *See page 5 of the instructions for limitations for automobiles.*)

23a   Do you have evidence to support the business/investment use claimed? ☐ **Yes** ☐ **No**   23b   If "Yes," is the evidence written? ☐ **Yes** ☐ **No**

(a) Type of property (list vehicles first)	(b) Date placed in service	(c) Business/ investment use percentage	(d) Cost or other basis	(e) Basis for depreciation (business/investment use only)	(f) Recovery period	(g) Method/ Convention	(h) Depreciation deduction	(i) Elected section 179 cost
24 Property used more than 50% in a qualified business use (See page 5 of the instructions.):								
		%						
		%						
		%						
25 Property used 50% or less in a qualified business use (See page 5 of the instructions.):								
		%			S/L –			
		%			S/L –			
		%			S/L –			

26   Add amounts in column (h). Enter the total here and on line 20, page 1 . . . . . **26**

27   Add amounts in column (i). Enter the total here and on line 7, page 1 . . . . **27**

Section B—Information on Use of Vehicles

Complete this section for vehicles used by a sole proprietor, partner, or other "more than 5% owner," or related person.

If you provided vehicles to your employees, first answer the questions in Section C to see if you meet an exception to completing this section for those vehicles.

	(a) Vehicle 1		(b) Vehicle 2		(c) Vehicle 3		(d) Vehicle 4		(e) Vehicle 5		(f) Vehicle 6	
28 Total business/investment miles driven during the year (DO NOT include commuting miles)												
29 Total commuting miles driven during the year												
30 Total other personal (noncommuting) miles driven												
31 Total miles driven during the year. Add lines 28 through 30.												
	Yes	No	Yes	No	Yes	No	Yes	No	Yes	No	Yes	No
32 Was the vehicle available for personal use during off-duty hours?												
33 Was the vehicle used primarily by a more than 5% owner or related person?												
34 Is another vehicle available for personal use?												

Section C—Questions for Employers Who Provide Vehicles for Use by Their Employees

*Answer these questions to determine if you meet an exception to completing Section B for vehicles used by employees who **are not** more than 5% owners or related persons.*

	Yes	No
35 Do you maintain a written policy statement that prohibits all personal use of vehicles, including commuting, by your employees?		
36 Do you maintain a written policy statement that prohibits personal use of vehicles, except commuting, by your employees? See page 6 of the instructions for vehicles used by corporate officers, directors, or 1% or more owners		
37 Do you treat all use of vehicles by employees as personal use?		
38 Do you provide more than five vehicles to your employees, obtain information from your employees about the use of the vehicles, and retain the information received?		
39 Do you meet the requirements concerning qualified automobile demonstration use? See page 6 of the instructions . .		

Note: *If your answer to 35, 36, 37, 38, or 39 is "Yes," you need not complete Section B for the covered vehicles.*

Part VI   Amortization

(a) Description of costs	(b) Date amortization begins	(c) Amortizable amount	(d) Code section	(e) Amortization period or percentage	(f) Amortization for this year
40 Amortization of costs that begins during your 19___ tax year:					
41 Amortization of costs that began before 19___ **41**					
42 **Total.** Enter here and on "Other Deductions" or "Other Expenses" line of your return . . . **42**					

✪ *Printed on recycled paper*

Chapter Five

Investment Formats

"If Patrick Henry thought that taxation without representation was bad, he should see how bad it is with representation."

—*Old Farmer's Almanac*

In this section, I'm going to bring up many ideas that are not put together in a linear manner. I intend to help you grasp an overall idea of balancing your portfolio and building income. I have analyzed three different stages in the wealth accumulation process, and I will list these before we get into the different ways of structuring your affairs.

THREE STAGES OF WEALTH ACCUMULATION

First stage: Accumulation stage—you take an aggressive approach to building an asset base when you start a business. This happens many times with people who are in their 20s or 30s.

Second stage: Maintenance stage—people who are in their mid-40s. In this stage, they try to hang on to everything they've built up. Expenses dramatically increase, and hopefully their investments are paying off.

Third stage: Retirement—and 60s. The time when you spend what you have been accumulating all your life.

In our economy, these stages do not necessarily correspond with these specific ages. I wish it were that way, but I notice people in my seminars in their 60s and 70s acting like they are in their 20s and 30s—they're just getting started. They've worked their whole lives for someone else and then realize they have nothing for retirement. They also decide they want to get another job after they've had to reduce their standard of living.

The three different reasons for investing your money are: 1) investing to build cash flow, 2) investing to have tax write offs, and 3) investing for growth and appreciation of assets. Fit any investment into those three things and you don't need much money to get started. Stocks may produce dividends, but they don't produce tax write offs. Real estate has been another popular option. However, starting your own business can get you all three.

You may not be ready to be an investor. I believe an investor is someone who gives his money to someone else and then steps out of control of that investment. If you picture the act of writing out a check and giving that to your stockbroker—that is the very act putting you out of control of your money. You can get back in control by calling that stockbroker and saying, "Please sell." Otherwise, you are out of control. The reason real estate has been so popular is because the act of writing out a check and buying real estate puts you in control—you are the owner. Some people lose control by renting out the real estate they own.

YOU CAN'T GET RICH BEING OUT OF CONTROL

I believe people need to get a chunk of money to start out with. If you don't do that and you are continually working at a job for someone else, then you need to determine where you are in the wealth accumulation stage. Contrary to what people teach, I believe the number one concern should be in building up your cash flow/monthly income. From a financial point of view, everything you invest in, property you buy, et cetera, needs to be judged by its ability to produce cash flow. If you are good at building your cash flow, you can use that money for future investments. If those investments pan out, you can perpetuate the cycle and keep it growing so you won't run out of money. Far too many people get caught up in investments that don't produce monthly checks. Only real estate, owning your own business, and a few other forms of investments produce monthly checks. Because we live in a "monthly check" society, you need to get monthly checks coming in to pay the bills.

INVEST FOR CASH FLOW

CASH-TO-ASSET-TO-CASH

A book I read stated that in the United States, there are 4.4 million families busy working that could be retired at an average income of $35,000 a year, if they would re-allocate their assets into investments producing more income.

This cash-to-asset-to-cash concept will be new to some of you. If you need to build up your asset base, you need to get your money back to cash. Sometimes that involves selling an investment; for example, buying stock that goes from one point to another point and immediately selling—don't wait for it to keep going. Capitalize on your profits, take your money, and buy some more. The longer your money is tied up, the more strapped you'll be. From an investment point of view, if you're going to balance your portfolio, you'll need to avoid debt like the plague. There is nothing that hurts businesses more. Lack of start-up capital to run a business causes debt because you mortgage your house, acquire loans, and so on.

OWN YOUR OWN BUSINESS

There is nothing better to accumulate wealth besides owning your own business. With your own business, you can buy and do for yourself many things you cannot do as an individual. Corporations can pay for insurance, cars, et cetera. Internally, within a business, you have a rate of growth. You can eventually sell it or take on partners. The best piece of advice about running a business is always know your exit before you go in the entrance. It's easy to go into business, but it's hard to get out of business; it's easy to get into real estate, but it's hard to get out of real estate; it's easy to get into personal relationships, but it's hard to get out of personal relationships. Always know what you want to do.

KNOW YOUR EXIT BEFORE YOU GO IN THE ENTRANCE

You have three choices to end a business: 1) close the doors; 2) don't end the ownership, just end your participation; and 3) sell it. You can structure your affairs in the way you want your business run. If you know you are going to sell, you'll do certain things to get it ready to be sold. Always stay a step ahead.

AVOID COSTLY ENTANGLEMENTS

I am not a big fan of partnerships. If you are going to enter into a partnership, do it in some kind of corporate fashion where you and your partner both own stock in the corporation. People say one thing and do another. I know of only one partnership in the Northwest where the partners are still friends. What you may agree upon now can change later.

LOOK FOR VALUE

Another way to create wealth is to keep looking for value. Stocks and bonds sometimes sell at distressed prices. I have an active IRA account and it does well. Every year around April 14, I'm asked to buy some new type of investment from my brokerage house. About eight years ago, I had to sell one of my IRAs. I had purchased a $2,000 investment in a Limited Partnership. About seven months later, I had to sell it and got back $600. I started thinking that whoever sold this is going to make commissions on both sides. I wondered if there are any other Limited Partnership units out there.

Over the next few months, when I was ready to put back in the $2,000, I made an offer on two units at $1,000 each—other people had purchased them and were selling them at a substantial discount to recover their cash. We are talking about bottom fishing here. I have a good friend who talks about a crustacean principle. He says if you think about crustaceans (shrimp, lobster), they eat all the garbage on the bottom of the sea and then turn into delicacies. This is the same idea if you are talking about buying wholesale and selling retail. Why not study and look at angles to buy things under market?

BOTTOM FISHING FOR INVESTMENTS

You need to understand where you are so you can time the sale of your good and bad investments and maximize the tax angles available to you. Find a good CPA or tax attorney and ask their advice. Keeping a lot of your profits comes down to a matter of timing.

LAW OF LEVERAGE

Let's talk about the law of leverage. If you are going to get wealthy, you have to increase your asset base—you have to control more assets. Buying a $20,000 second mortgage is a form of leverage. You are trading cash for a larger asset that is usually earning a higher interest rate. Starting up your business with very little cash is a form of leverage. You can get a high rate of return from a small invested dollar.

ACCELERATE YOUR EARNING POWER

The last point comes from a book called *Honest Business*. For this book, the author interviewed 100 millionaires and asked this question: "How did you make it?" Of the 100 asked, one thing was clear: they were experts in their own field; they

REAL ESTATE SHOULD
HAVE A SUFFICIENT
PLACE IN YOUR
PORTFOLIO

weren't necessarily good investors. If you can become an expert in a financial field that has a high rate of return you have a double-edged sword. If you don't have a field, I recommend real estate—investing in second mortgages and start-up companies. The University of Michigan conducted a detailed study and determined most of the wealthiest people in America had a substantial part of their assets in real estate. However, these people were not real estate investors (buying, renting, et cetera). They owned other types of businesses, but a substantial part of their asset base was the real estate the buildings were sitting on.

We all want our retirements to be healthy and wealthy, but the best way to get there is to have a balanced approach, and the balancing should be done in favor of cash flow—building up those groupings of investments that produce monthly checks. If you do that, you'll be happier today and tomorrow. One more thing to realize is that your money will take on your personality. If you are aggressive, your money will be aggressive. If you are laid back, your money will be laid back.

STOCK MARKET INVESTORS

Are there any tax strategies you can employ while investing in the stock market? If you make a profit, you'll have to claim it as received. If you buy stock for $50 and sell it for $60, you have a $10 capital gain to claim. This becomes part of your portfolio income, which affects your active income,

TIMING = SAVINGS

but it's really kept in a separate account. You can have all your stock investments, all your winners and losers playing against each other. Here are a few strategies you should consider:

1) You can time the sale of your investments. Specifically, if you have an investment you are considering selling, maybe you'll want to sell in November

or December if you're losing money and you need losses for the year. However, a stock may be at a high price and rather than selling on December 20th and having to take the profits this year, consider selling eleven or twelve days later to move the profits into next year. You would have your profits and a whole year to offset them with other types of deductions.

2) You can have your stock market investments owned by different legal entities. *[Note: one of the concerns of having a corporation own stock market investments is to make sure it's not considered a holding corporation, which falls under the banking rules. If a corporation is just in existence to own assets in the stock market, it will probably be a holding corporation. However, if the corporation has rental properties, purchased notes, mortgages, business interests, other limited partnerships, or directly owns different businesses and minority or majority positions of stock in other corporations that own businesses, and also has a brokerage account on the side—then it definitely would not be considered a holding corporation.]* By having two or three different corporate entities running your enterprises and investments, each one owns stock in the stock market. Then you have lessened the amount you would have to pay, and you have also lessened your exposure to risk by not having all of your eggs in one basket.

> **DIVERSIFY YOUR ENTITIES**

3) We are always faced with "when" to claim profits as profits. You could buy a mutual fund or a stock and sell that particular group of stocks at a certain point in time. If you are constantly

buying and selling stocks in one particular corporation, then the IRS would usually take the last in and the first out. You have two ways of claiming this: LIFO or FIFO, which is last in, first out or first in, first out. If you bought 100 shares of stock, the IRS would want to look at this, decide which of the stocks was purchased at a lower price and which is being sold right now. They want to take and calculate the largest capital gain. However, if you have documented that you are selling a group of stocks which you have the documentation for—it would stand the test and prove that the stocks you are selling were purchased on the date you stated. It's good to sell the stock in the blocks you purchased them, therefore keep track of when you purchased them. Mark the sale on the same piece of paper and keep good records of all of these transactions.

KEEP GOOD RECORDS

Another strategy for investing in the stock market is a corporate strategy. Specifically, it's the 70% exclusion rule. If you own stock in the market and you receive dividends, 100% of those dividends are going to be taxed to you.

I'm amazed that there are still a few people out there who believe if they have their stock involved in a dividend reinvestment program, and they actually do not receive the dividends, they won't have to claim that dividend as income. I still have people coming to my seminars and when I ask how many of them get dividends, they say, "I don't get them because I don't want to pay taxes on them, so I just have the dividends reinvested into more stock on a quarterly basis through a company dividend reinvestment program." This is naiveté at its extreme. Whether you receive the money or not, the IRS is still going to claim that this has been a constructive receipt of dividends and you'll have to claim them as income. The point is, you have to claim 100% of dividends as income if they are paid to you as an individual.

THE EXCLUSION RULE

Do not own your stock brokerage account as an individual. Have your family corporation own the brokerage account. Let's look at the implications. If your corporation owns stock in another corporation, that corporation pays a dividend to your corporation into your brokerage account. Upon receipt of that, your corporation gets to ignore 70% of the dividend income. It does not have to claim that income. It's as though it did not exist. All your company has to claim is 30%.

The following is an example. You have taken in $1,000. That money can go into your corporate checking account; it can be used to pay bills or buy a new car for you. Your corporation has taken in the money, but it only has to claim 30% (or $300) of that money as income. The remaining 70% of the dividend income paid from one corporation to another is excluded from taxation.

A lot of you are probably thinking, "Why didn't my CPA tell me this?" I'm going to ask you that question too. At my seminars, I ask, "Why did you have to come here and learn this from a former cab driver? Why didn't your CPA tell you this?"

Most people shout, "They just don't know." And that's true.

I want to isolate this small amount of money from the aforementioned example to prove a point. You've taken in a check from the XYZ company for $1,000; all you have to claim is $300, but you've taken in $1,000. You could use that $1,000 on expenses, therefore paying out $1,000. You have

$1,000 in expenses and $300 in income. Look at what your bottom line is—a $700 loss. I have shown you how to create a $700 loss. Most of you are just taking in the $1,000, claiming the whole thing, and paying taxes on the entire amount.

RECEIVE MONEY AND
ONLY CLAIM PART OF IT

I hope you see the value in this simple, yet powerful investment strategy. From a stock market point of view, investing in dividends allows you to receive a lot of money from them. Specifically, look at companies that are paying high dividends—but only worry about claiming 30% of it as income. You have to ask yourself, "Does Mobil Oil own stock in AT&T? Does AT&T own stock in IBM?" The answer is, "Yes." They own stock in other companies. They have their own brokerage accounts because their tax preparers realize they can build up a substantial amount of income and only have to worry about claiming 30% of that as income.

If you like this 70% exclusion rule, you must realize "S" Corporations do not qualify for this rule. Only "C" Corporations or regular, ordinary corporations qualify. (For further explanation on the difference between "S" and "C" Corporations, see the *Incorporation Handbook*.)

TWO TYPES
AVAILABLE

INVESTING WITH ANNUITIES

Annuities are usually life insurance company products. Simply put, they work like this: you put your money in now, and you get it out later in the form of monthly or annual checks. There are basically two types of annuities.

1) *Fixed*—Your money is placed into fixed income-type investments, like bonds, that grow at a fixed rate.

2) *Variable*—You control where the money goes.

    a) You have "sub-accounts" and the growth of your investments depends on how well you do at choosing the different investment vehicles available.

b) All this money is accumulated tax free—until it's withdrawn.

c) The fees for managing these taxes are much more expensive than a mutual fund.

d) Some have high 12b (1) charges (from .033 to 1.75%).

The money put in is not deductible. It would be better to put more into an IRA, SEP-IRA or pension.

Who should use variable annuities? If you are in a high tax bracket (28% or over) and know you'll be in a lower bracket later, then these are good investments. Don't use these if you need the money in the next decade; there is a 10% penalty upon withdrawal, plus taxes due.

MAXIMIZING THE PROGRAMS AVAILABLE FOR COLLEGE TUITION

Children can own investments indirectly through their parents or a guardian. These investments could be held in a trust or some other custodial account.

SAVING FOR CHILDREN

Prior to the age of 14, a child has no income tax on the first $600 of unearned income. On the next $600, the money is taxed only 15%. If, however, the child has unearned income in excess of $1,200, that income is taxed at the parent's rate. What this means is the first $1,200 of portfolio-type income only incurs a $90 tax—or 15% of $600. If that money was taxed at the parent's rate of 36%, the amount owed to the IRS would be $216. Once a child turns 14, he or she continues to avoid federal taxes on the first $600 of unearned income, but the next $21,450 of unearned income is taxed at a maximum rate of 15% (this is the tax bracket for single filers). It is controlling investments made by and income received from those investments between the ages of one and 14 where the most serious tax advantage can occur if properly structured.

BONDS FOR COLLEGE

One thing you can do is invest in United States series EE Savings Bonds. Interest earned on these bonds grows tax deferred until they are redeemed. The interest rates earned on these can never be less than 4% and the income is free of state and local tax, as long as the parent's adjusted gross income is less than $60,000 (as of 1993, this amount is adjusted annually). The only way this interest becomes tax free is if these bonds are used to pay for tuition and books—college room and board does not qualify for this. The interest on these bonds could be partially or entirely free depending on how they are used. *[Note: this exemption from paying income tax is applicable only if the parents own the bonds.]*

The only drawback to these kinds of bonds is they may not keep pace with inflation especially since college inflation has been going up at such a dramatic pace compared to overall inflation.

There are many other arrangements that can be made under the Uniform Gift to Minor Act (UGMA). Parents can set up trusts for children and those trusts can invest in more traditional investments. However, there are serious tax consequences on trusts of this nature—the tax brackets shoot up to 39.6% on all earnings over $7,500. But if you combine your desire to have college tuition set aside with strategies to structure your family's affairs, you can continually outpace inflation with good investments held in different entities which allow for maximum tax deductions and write offs.

Chapter Six

Structuring Your Affairs

"There's nothing more dangerous than the U.S. Congress with an idea."

—E. Patrick McGuire of the conference Board (Opening a conference examining tax incentives)

I'm going to make two assumptions: you are either making pretty good money and want to learn how to keep more of it (for example, by saving money on taxes), or you are just starting out, either in your own business or as an investor, and you want to learn ways to structure your affairs to save money on taxes in the long run.

Either way, I'd like to start out by mentioning I believe Ronald Reagan's approach to tax reduction strategies is the best one around. His strategy summed up could be this: make more money, quit worrying about tax loop holes, quit worrying about tax shelter type investments and get on with making more money, lower the tax brackets in order to encourage people to make more.

Tax Brackets

With that in mind, let's talk about the brackets and see if we can work those brackets to help you keep more. Because the tax laws are always changing, it's hard to give out the actual amounts. If you are a married person filing jointly and you're making between $0 and

> **Work the brackets**

$41,200 a year, you are going to be in a 15% tax bracket. Money made between $41,200 and $99,600 a year is going to put you in a 28% tax bracket. Anything over that amount throws you into a 31 to 36%, and even a 39.6% bracket. I think that there is an over-looked angle to making money. It's very simple—quit making money as one entity. Instead of making money as one person, start making money as a person and a business. For example, let's say you are making around $70,000 a year. If you were making that as a sole proprietor, you would be taxed 15% on $41,200 and 28% on the remaining $28,800.

Split this money in half and make it in two different entities: a corporation making $35,000 a year is taxed in a 15% tax bracket. The other $35,000, if made yourself, is in a 15% tax bracket. Now look at what we just did. We saved 13%, which is a difference between the 15 or 28%, on the $28,800— or about $3,800 this year. Every year we can save a like amount by simply dividing up your business entities. This could be done with two different corporations, or with a sole proprietorship and a corporation, or as a person paying off fees to another corporation. There are many different angles to this.

USE DIFFERENT ENTITIES

Let me give you another angle on structuring your financial affairs. You are a company and you contract with another company to provide management, consulting, and marketing services for you or your company. You pay a fee to that company for providing these services. This is one way of moving money from one company to another, legally. Your CPA can help you structure your affairs to make sure everything is done properly. You have just lessened the tax burden in one entity by moving the money to another and paying it out as a legitimate business expense. Essentially, you are operating two different companies.

You can directly/indirectly own or control the other business enterprise. It will have a different Federal ID number, a different address, and possibly different owners (including different year-ends, et cetera).

One other point: this strategy is used extensively by companies which have corporate income tax rates based on the net profit of a corporation. Who wouldn't want to move $50,000 in expenses out of California (which taxes it at 12%) to Nevada where there is no state tax? Let me diagram this:

NEVADA = NO
STATE TAXES

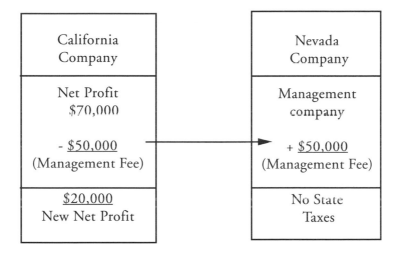

California Company	Nevada Company
Net Profit $70,000	Management company
- $50,000 (Management Fee)	+ $50,000 (Management Fee)
$20,000 New Net Profit	No State Taxes

Many people have used this tactic to convert rental income, which is not subject to social security taxes, but which, on the other hand, does not factor into the percentage of money which can go into a Pension Plan, into earned income. A person with a number of rental properties may pay out fees (rental management fees) to another company, lessening the profits on the rental properties, but putting that money into another company and making that money available for an exclusion into retirement accounts.

CAPITAL GAINS—ACTIVE OR PASSIVE

What about capital? It is either active or passive. If you bought IBM stock for $55 and sold it for $65, you made $10 per share of active capital gain. If you bought rental real estate for $150,000 and sold it for $300,000, that would be a passive capital gain. The easiest way to think about this is to relate it to two different swimming pools—the types of investment income and losses are calculated against each other. All active income and losses are calculated against each other. All passive income and losses are calculated against each other. They don't mix.

BUSINESS CALCULATIONS

A great way to save money on taxes is to have your own business, whether it is a corporation or sole proprietorship. A lot of bills can be deducted from life insurance, medical insurance, and board of directors meetings in different places around the country. I believe if you are going to be in business, you should be a corporation. Sole proprietorships are dangerous. Many people call me and are in trouble because they are vulnerable to lawsuits and have not set up a corporation.

If you are a corporation, working the tax brackets is really important. Corporations can have all kinds of expenses, and they can do a lot of things for you which you can't do for yourself.

DOUBLE TAXATION

People are afraid of double taxation, which is simply this: the corporation cannot deduct dividends and the individual who receives dividends is going to have to pay taxes on that income, therefore double taxation. If the money is taken out as a salary or bonus, these are tax deductible items to the "C" corporation. There are three circumstances where you may want to consider being an "S" corporation:

1) Rental real estate

2) Small group investment

3) Any high cash flow business (over $125,000 a year), if you have other losses.

"S" corporations are very limited in what they can deduct. The best way to save money is to use your own brain power: study and research. You pay for education once, you continually pay for ignorance.

I'M NOT BIG ON 'S' CORPORATIONS

OWNERSHIP-CONTROL-INCOME

Many people who come to my seminars are worried about the implications of lawsuits and erosion of their asset values due to excessive taxation. They are worried about passing along all their assets to their children. They want to live the good life, and yet they see how exclusions by the government are going to affect them. They also realize we live in a trigger-happy lawsuit society.

There are four questions you need to ask yourself when setting up your legal entities. 1) Who is going to own them? 2) In what format are they going to own them? 3) Who is going to control the entity? 4) Who will receive the income and in what manner?

As Americans, we believe everything has to be even. We believe, if you own 50% of a company, you are entitled to 50% of that company—50% of the ownership and 50% of the cash flow. Nothing could be further from the truth. The real truth is you could own 1% of the company, control 75% and be entitled to 65% of the cash flow. Ownership, control and cash flow have nothing to do with each other.

Once you understand this concept, every time you set up a legal entity you need to ask yourself, "Who is going to own it? Who is going to control it? How will it be run? Who is going to get the income and how will it be paid out?" Realize that once you see these could be diverse percentages, all kinds of things become possible. You can literally own $1/100$ of 1%

of a company and control 100% of it. But since your ownership is so small, you could keep your estate really small, while controlling a multi-million dollar enterprise.

YOU CAN CONTROL WITH VERY LITTLE OWNERSHIP

I ask people at my seminars, "Let's say you're worth $1 million, how much of that (what percentage) would you like put at risk to avoid losing the whole thing?" Most people do not have $1 million tied up in one asset. If they are worth a million dollars, this usually involves several hundred thousand dollars in a business enterprise and perhaps several hundred thousand dollars in real estate owned by the enterprise. It may involve one or two hundred thousand dollars in brokerage accounts. Again, the question I ask is, "What percentage of this money would you like to have at risk?"

A lot of them say, "None."

You really can't say none. If you're not willing to put a small percentage of this money at risk, you risk losing the whole thing. Compare it to gangrene. If you get gangrene in your foot and you're not willing to cut off that foot, you could risk losing your leg or even your whole life. If you're not willing to risk losing a small percentage, you stand the chance of losing everything. With this in mind, I came up with Rules A and B.

RULE A

Rule A is what I call the 20% Rule. Whatever your net worth is, no more than 20% of your total should be owned in one legal entity. For example, if your net worth is $1 million, you could set up some corporations. Corporation #1 would be worth $180,000—this is made by buying and selling properties. You set up Corporation #2 worth $240,000. This corporation is purchasing notes and mortgages and it has interest income. You have a Limited Partnership worth

MY 20% RULE

$220,000. That $220,000 is the equity in rental properties. Corporation #3 is worth $160,000. This corporation is a dry cleaning business you own.

Another Limited Partnership, which has some rental properties, is worth $200,000. It's never going to be exactly even because your equities and assets are going up and down in value. All this adds up to about one million dollars. Out of the blue, someone comes into your dry cleaning business, gets hurt on one of your machines, and claims you are negligent. They are suing you and the insurance will not cover the damages. That corporation may be forced into bankruptcy.

Let's say the dry cleaning business was owned in your own name and somebody were to come in and sue—that little rotten apple could contaminate all the others in the bushel. You could risk losing everything because you could have liens against you from that dry cleaning business which could be attached to all of your rental real estate, your personal residence, and so on.

Rule A specifically says no more than 20% should be owned in one particular entity. Each one of these corporations has its own tax bracket; each limited partnership has the money flowing down to the different owners—which could be different from partnership to partnership.

DIVIDE AND CONQUER

RULE B
Rule B is for people just starting out. First you set up one corporation, and when that corporation gets to be worth $150,000 to $200,000 in investments or equities, you set up another corporation. Let's say you grow a corporation until it's worth $150,000 to $200,000. You need tax write offs at that time, but you want to own them through a Limited Partnership. A Limited Partnership would buy rental properties worth $150,000 to $200,000. If you want to keep

buying more, set up another Limited Partnership. You grow in leaps and bounds like this, and you do not accumulate all your wealth in one legal entity.

After following Rule A or B, and creating several, different legal entities, you could create a parent corporation. (For further explanation, see Chapter Seven.) You could have these different entities paying money to each other for providing services for each other. This is another way of moving money from one year to the next and one entity to the next, to lessen the tax bite.

CONTROL THE ENTITIES THAT OWN YOUR INVESTMENTS

Chapter Seven

Corporate Strategies

"Where deductions are based on a number of small items not susceptible to complete documentary substantiation, reasonable determinations should be made at the district examination level. Consideration will always be given to the reasonableness of the taxpayers' claimed deductions."

—*Policy Statement P4-39*

I've had the distinct opportunity for the last several years to travel the country from the Atlantic to the Pacific as well as foreign countries and speak about the values of making money in this country. I really believe we can do a lot more if we have a little more money coming in. One of the ways of doing that, as I've said before, is to be in business. Many years ago, I categorized and designed some angles to making money with real estate investments by treating real estate as a business, rather than an investment. I was able to make a lot of money, and countless thousands of other people have also benefited from these ideas.

Three Aspects Of Investments

There are really two ways of tapping the full potential of three main aspects of investments (cash flow, tax write offs and growth). All forms of investment look for these three things, but only with real estate or owning your own business can you tap all three at the same time and get started with very little money.

> Cash flow, tax write offs and growth

If you can combine real estate and business (or some other angles to the stock market) and use them like a business, then you get the best of both worlds. Later on in this chapter I will cover what this has to do with setting up a corporation.

WATCH WHAT RICH PEOPLE DO

Let's talk about corporations in general, and then I'll couple that with the strength of incorporating in Nevada to show you how powerful it really can be. Many years ago a very wise man told me, "If you really want to get rich in this country, watch what poor people do and don't do it." I've taken that to heart. I've watched poor people all over the country. What they do, simply put, is not going to make them a lot of money. The other side of that coin if you want to make a lot of money, watch what rich people do and do what they do.

Here are some strategies for you to consider in relationship to building a business, whether you are in business, a consultant, or working for someone else.

CORPORATIONS ARE BEST

Corporations are simply the best alternative. I wish I could sit here and say, "You have three choices: a, b, and c. Choice 'a' is a sole proprietorship, choice 'b' is some form of a partnership or joint venture, and choice 'c' is a corporation." But it's not that simple. Because of liability consequences, tax planning, lawsuit protection, et cetera, partnerships (general) and sole proprietorships lack so much, and there really is no other choice than to incorporate.

SOLE PROPRIETORSHIPS

Let's explore why sole proprietorships are a bad option. With a sole proprietorship you have no liability protection whatsoever. If you own a dry cleaning business or a pet store and somebody comes in, gets hurt, and sues, they are not suing the business, they are suing you. They can get liens against your property and wreak all kinds of havoc in your life with judgments.

Sole proprietorships afford absolutely no lawsuit or tax protection. All of the money you make in your business is taxed directly to you; it goes right on to your Form 1040. So coupled with your other sources of income, there is no way to minimize the tax consequences.

AVOID SOLE PROPRIETORSHIPS

I've had the unique opportunity to sit in my office and talk to people on the phone. Most of the phone calls coming in are people who have problems, are getting sued, or getting killed on taxes and they want to know how to structure their affairs to avoid these kinds of problems. Almost always their call is about problems in the past tense. The most frequent thing I hear is, "Wade, I went to your seminar four or eight years ago, and I heard you talk about corporations and pension plans way back then. I went out and started a business and didn't do that. Now I'm going through a lawsuit or a bankruptcy." Or, "I'm making too much money and I'm going to get killed on taxes. What am I going to do? Had I taken your advice way back then, I wouldn't be in this situation right now."

So my point again, watch what rich people do. Watch what big corporations do. The little corporations out there should copy as many things about big corporations as they can. Structure your affairs like they structure their affairs, and you'll find that you can make more money and keep more of what you're making.

WHY INCORPORATE?

Why incorporate? First of all, you have now created another entity. Instead of making the money as yourself, you are making the money as a second, third, or fourth entity. If you have different businesses, different investments or groupings of investments, you may want to put them under different legal entities. Why? One of the big reasons to split up your different businesses or assets into different entities is to avoid lawsuits that could come to one entity. When I talk about limiting liability in a corporation, there are two aspects I would like to mention. One of the liability limitations is for the directors and officers of the corporation. The second one is in regard to the shareholders of the corporation.

An officer or director of a corporation is not responsible for the activities of the corporation unless they do something illegal. They can be guilty of malfeasance, misfeasance, or fraud, but other than that they are not directly responsible for the activities of the corporation. The corporation is a separate entity. Shareholders are completely protected from liability. By owning stock in a company you are in no way, shape, or form responsible for the activities of the corporation.

YOU HAVE ANOTHER ENTITY WORKING FOR YOU

Do you remember a few years back when Union Carbide had a major disaster in Bhopal, India? The only way the shareholders were hurt in that fiasco was when the value of the stock went down for a short period of time. Not one shareholder was sued for the activities of the corporation. The corporation went through many lawsuits. They lost a lot of money, but as they built their asset base and cash flow back up, the value of the stock came back. The point is that the veil of the corporation was not penetrated. None of the contestants in the lawsuit went directly after the owners of the corporation. So being an owner through stock or share ownership does not make share owners directly responsible for any of the activities.

SHAREHOLDERS ARE NOT DIRECTLY RESPONSIBLE

The example I just used is in a publicly charted corporation. The same holds true in private corporations. The individual shareholders, which could be your family members, friends, or any other extended family members, are not directly responsible for the activities of the corporation.

CONTROLLED GROUPS

In regard to corporate tax strategies, I have consistently mentioned multiple corporations—having one corporation running a dry cleaning business, another corporation owning real estate, another buying notes and mortgages, and all these corporations having their own brokerage accounts. And yet another parent, control, or management corporation can move money out of a particular state with a management or consulting fee to lessen the tax bite from direct state taxes. One of the problems with this is if you own or control the stock of these two or three different corporations, the IRS will treat them as one if they feel it is necessary. They can conduct a pretty extensive search in tracking down who controls the stock directly and indirectly. So there needs to be big caution on ownership. Also realize there are other entities available, such as a Family Limited Partnership and the two different types of corporations—"S" and "C." (You still have the ability, in a minor way, of having a sole proprietorship making money which could draw money out of the corporations.)

You need to be aware that there could be a control group question, and any CPA should be able to help you structure your affairs to minimize any consequences here. Make sure all of your monies made in these different entities are taxed at the lowest possible rate.

Another reason for being a corporation is for estate purposes. Within a corporation you can have varied ownership. You are starting a brand new company and you and your spouse each take 5% of the stock, and you give each of your three children 30% of the stock. As this company grows to be worth

$2 million and the father dies, only 5% of the $2 million shows up in his personal estate. Five percent of $2 million is $100,000. He is well within his $600,000, one time exclusion.

A LIVING TRUST COUPLED WITH A CORPORATION IS DYNAMIC

Corporations are way ahead of Living Trusts in this manner. A Living Trust cannot do this. Living Trusts are wonderful, but they are limited in what they can do. However, a Living Trust coupled with a corporation is a dynamic combination because the Living Trust will take control of that stock Mom and Dad own in the corporation and move it all, through death, to avoid probate. So you can move assets from generation to generation. With a corporation, you own a small amount of stock, control it (because the voting rights are controlled by the parents), and all of the value of the corporation will eventually go to the children. You are passing along millions of dollars of value to your children, and you can do all this through a simple family corporation.

CONTROL

When you set up your corporation, you can totally maintain control of your different investments and different businesses. The point I've made at my seminars around the country is that you don't need to own anything, but you need to control everything. Your stock has the voting rights in the company. The voting stock votes on who the directors are going to be, and then the directors choose the officers.

HAVE ANNUAL MEETINGS—MAKE THEM FUN

If you are going to be a legitimate corporation, you need to have annual meetings. They can be done in your office or another place of your choosing. In this meeting you'll list the time and place, who is present, what you've agreed to do, what the purpose of the business is, and discuss any problems or concerns of the business. These meetings, which many people shy away from, are really quite simple and can be a lot of fun and give a lot of direction to the company.

To reiterate, with a corporation you have another entity; you have split up your assets for liability purposes; you have great tax benefits; you have estate planning benefits that are afforded by no other legal entity; and you are in total control.

> **NEVADA IS UNEQUIVOCALLY THE BEST STATE FOR INCORPORATING**

NEVADA

Let's throw this whole thing into high gear and talk about what Nevada has brought to the business arena. Obviously there is a difference in incorporating in the various states. Why Nevada?

1) Nevada is dedicated to becoming the number one state. They want everyone to incorporate there. Every day, in the state of Nevada, there are more corporations filed than in all the other 49 states put together. Nevada has become the number one state for incorporating. Why? In Nevada there is no corporate tax, no stock transfer tax, no succession tax, no franchise tax. There are no taxes whatsoever in the state of Nevada. Many companies open up satellite offices there and have their satellite offices running the major businesses back in their own home state. A lot of companies have bank accounts there. It has become a safe haven for corporations all over the country and even all over the world because of this "no tax" situation.

2) In the State of Nevada the officers and directors of the company cannot be sued for the activities of the corporation. It is virtually impossible to sue the directors, especially if they are "famous." In

most states, doing business as an individual is not the same as doing business as a corporation, and anyone you do business with cannot and should not sue you personally for the activities of the corporation. That is why so many companies are incorporating. They realize, from a liability point of view, that no other state affords total protection like Nevada.

3) Nevada is the only state which has not signed an information-sharing agreement with the IRS. You've heard the term reciprocity, or having a "reciprocal agreement." There is no such agreement signed with the IRS. When I teach my seminars, a lot of people clap and cheer in the back of the room. My personal feeling is we should do everything in compliance with all state and federal laws. Usually the IRS will use the state's records. A lot of people will file their IRS returns, but they do not file their state returns. So the states just get access to the IRS returns and use that information to go after the people for the tax owed to the state—but not so in Nevada. In Nevada, there is no reciprocity whatsoever with the IRS.

NO RECIPROCITY WITH THE IRS

4) You can have several different special classes of stock.

5) The State of Nevada has the most liberal security laws in the whole country. If you want to take your company public, Nevada is one of the best states to do that from in terms of registration, so it's easier to take the company into the public arena.

6) The officers of the corporation are afforded the broadest corporate powers available. By simply writing something into the articles of incorporation or into the by-laws of the corporation, the direction of the corporation can be determined, the different business activities can be changed, and different classes of stock can be added or subtracted.

> OFFICERS HAVE BROAD CORPORATE POWERS

7) Anyone or any entity can own stock in a Nevada corporation. Foreigners can own stock in a Nevada Corporation.

8) In the State of Nevada there is absolutely no minimum capital required to start up. You can start up a corporation with no money whatsoever.

> NO MINIMUM CAPITAL REQUIRED

OTHER CORPORATE STRATEGIES

Let me give you a few other corporate strategies to consider. First of all, you can put in the maximum allowed in a Pension Plan faster in a corporation than you can in a sole proprietorship. The percentage is larger and because it is larger, the amount it is based on is smaller and you can put aside the maximum amount faster. Next, if you decide to use my company in Nevada, I'm going to give you one clever way to structure your affairs. It is sophisticated, but not hard to understand.

Think back when we discussed having another entity. Now I'm going to show you how you can have another entity and use it in a way to really help you save some money on taxes and avoid the other things that can go wrong—like lawsuits to one company. You now have two corporations, and you can even use our office in Nevada. We have a set-up where we are not only your resident agent, but we can even rent you office space. We have copy machines there, conference rooms, fax machines—the whole works. We'll even help you get your bank account. Your company in Tennessee, California, New York, Florida, or wherever can contract with this Nevada corporation for management, consulting, or marketing services and pay a fee to that company for providing these services. These fees could be flat fees, or fees based on performance, it could be a percentage of your sales. This fee is paid to the Nevada company.

Now remember in the state of Nevada, there are no corporate taxes, and this Nevada corporation could buy a car for you, a small truck, and other business equipment; it could pay for seminars in Hawaii that you need to go to and sharpen your business skills. This corporation in Nevada can operate on its own. You've moved money, as an expense, from your existing state into Nevada. Therefore you have taken the money out of a potentially high income tax state and put it into a state with no corporate taxes whatsoever. We are not trying to avoid any federal taxes here. You may, by the way, save a little on federal taxes because now, instead of having one corporation taxed at $70,000, you now have one corporation taxed at $35,000 and the other Nevada corporation taxed federally at $35,000. So you may save some money, but that is not the major purpose. The major purpose is to legitimately and legally avoid paying some taxes by having a separate corporation set up to provide real services to your other company.

CORPORATIONS AND LIVING TRUSTS

Another strategy is that a corporation, in conjunction with a Living Trust, makes a Living Trust a lot more "workable," or more realistic. The Living Trust is an entity that avoids probate. If your corporation stock is controlled by or owned by the Living Trust, you now have a really good way of controlling your company after you are gone. Wherein your trustee (the person you have handling your affairs after you are gone) can step in and with a minimum of effort, take over the cor-

No CORPORATE TAXES

poration and run everything for the benefit of your family. People ask me all the time, "Do you need a corporation or a Living Trust?"

I say, "You need both." You need a Living Trust to avoid probate, but you also need a corporation to structure your affairs so that everything is taken care of for your family.

Does the corporation own the Living Trust? Does the Living Trust own the corporation? These are other questions often asked by people. They are not one and the same. A Living Trust is a trust—an entity set up to avoid probate. A corporation is another legal entity basically set up to do economic things—run businesses and have investments. Particular stock in the corporation is owned by the Living Trust. You could still have a lot of stock in the company owned by your children, and if your children are older, their stock should be assigned to their Living Trust.

STOCK IN A CORPORATION CAN BE OWNED BY A LIVING TRUST

Do you see how they both work together? For example, you have a company you've worked many, many years to build. You don't want excessive taxation to shut down your business after you are gone. You make a wise decision to set up a Living Trust. The stock you own has been assigned to the Living Trust and shows up in Schedule "A" of the Living Trust. Upon your death, the trustee steps in and takes control of the stock, and its voting stock basically has control of the corporation. The transfer upon your death is really simple and easy to handle. So again, you need both a Living Trust and a corporation and in addition to that you should have your own retirement account set up and sponsored by the corporation.

TAKE TIME TO STRUCTURE YOUR AFFAIRS

Take time out to structure your affairs. Don't just read this information and think you can wait.

It would be better to have a corporation set up and not need it, than to need a corporation when you have a new business opportunity and not have one.

If your CPA or tax attorney needs this information, please share it with them. We work with a lot of CPAs and tax attorneys in helping them set up the financial affairs of their clients. They use us to do all the paperwork. I've tried to take the high cost out of education, and I've also tried to take the high cost out of setting up these entities.

YEAR-ENDS EXPLAINED

CORPORATE YEAR-ENDS

There are three different times of the year when you should consider having your corporate tax year-end. As a sole proprietorship, your only choice is December 31. This wreaks all kinds of havoc because everything you make personally in a job, and everything you make from a small company you're running part time, flows into the same tax year. You have everything in one tax bracket and in the same year. However, as a corporation, you can choose to have a different fiscal year-end. A very popular one that I see companies using is June 30th, but I cannot figure out why anybody would want to have a June 30th year-end. The two that I advocate strongly are January 31st and/or March 31st. Another one is October 31st, and we will cover that later.

Why January 31st? When you set up your corporation, you're allowed to choose your corporate year-end. Every corporation can, one time and one time only, declare what is called a "short year-end." This means it does not have to be in business the full twelve months to have its year-end determined. You could even set up a corporation in December, or even in the middle of January, and have its first year-end just a few weeks later—January 31st. Thereafter, the year would be exactly 365 days starting February 1st, and ending January 31st of the next year.

Let's say you start your company's business operating on February 1st. You make some profits in February, March, April, May, and then on through the summer and fall. If you were to pull out a large amount of money in December, it will be taxed within just a few short months. The corporation gets to deduct it as income, but you have to claim it as personal income. By receiving the money at the end of your tax year, you have no time to offset it with other tax deductible items. So, once again, you are at the mercy of having to claim income as income at the worst possible time.

> ALLOWS YOU TO CONTROL WHEN YOU CLAIM INCOME

But, in a corporate entity, you can have different year-ends, which allows you to do this: instead of pulling the money out in December, you wait until January to get the money out. If you do want to pull it out in December, one way to do so is to borrow the money from the corporation so that you do not have to claim it as income. The corporation is now making really good money and it can take a full eleven months of earning power before moving the money into January of the next year. You pick a date—January 10 or 15—and you pull the money out. Remember, not to pull the money out as dividends. Dividends are not tax deductible under the current laws. You pull the money out as a salary or bonus, because salaries and bonuses are tax deductible. The corporation now has a tax deduction of the money that it has paid you. You receive this money in January of the next year. When do you have to pay taxes on it? April 15th, of the following year, but notice when you received it. You received it in January, so now you have the ability to go out and purchase shelter-type investments and create tax deductions so that next April 15th, fifteen months later when you have to pay taxes, you can seriously minimize those taxes. A lot of people are saying, especially CPAs, "What about estimated taxes? What about quarterly taxes?" If you are subject to estimated quarterly taxes I have a few thoughts for you that I think are applicable:

1) Do not pull out all the money to one person. You may want to pull the money out to two or three different people—husband, wife, or children—to make sure that you are not making this money susceptible to estimated quarterly taxes.

PULL OUT MONEY TO DIFFERENT PEOPLE

2) If you are susceptible to estimated quarterly taxes, don't forget to take your estimated quarterly losses. I'm amazed at how many people are constantly being zapped by estimated taxes, when they may have rental properties or other tax-sheltered type investments. They use these investment deductions on an annual basis, but they forget or neglect to use them on a quarterly basis. If you fall into this category, remember to take your estimated quarterly deductions and losses and use them to minimize your taxes as you go along.

The main point is, you have taken one entity and have moved it from one year to the next. Think about it—what about J.C. Penney, Sears, and other big corporations? When do they have their corporate year-ends? Not December 31st. Most of these kinds of companies make the bulk of their money at Christmas time—the holiday shopping season. When do they pay out their store managers' bonuses and their regional managers' bonuses and all their employee benefits? They pay them out right before their corporate year-end. They don't particularly care when the employees receive the money, whether it is January, February or March, but what they want to do is get rid of these expenses before their corporate year-end to lessen their tax liability. If the big corporations can do it, then we can too. We have every right to look at what the big guys are doing and follow their lead. That extra five, ten, or fifteen thousand dollars your small company is going to save could mean a lot more to you on a percentage basis than a million dollars that Sears may be saving by employing the same strategy. This is a powerful tool.

Now let's get to March 31st. I think January 31st is the best, but it creates one problem. It is not on a calendar quarter. All the other forms you use, especially 940s, 941s, and other state income filing reports, are done on a calendar quarter basis (January-March; April-June; July-September; and October-December.) If you put your corporate year-end at March 31, obviously your corporate year begins on April 1st. You start out in April (once again) and you go along and make money. You only have eight months of earning power, not eleven before December 31st. But still, for the sake of simplicity, your CPAs and tax advisors will like March 31st much better because they do not have to work two sets of books for things that have to be filed on a quarterly basis. So March 31st is probably more advisable if you have employees, or are filling out numerous forms on a quarterly basis.

> **CALENDAR QUARTER MAY BE BEST**

OCTOBER 31ST YEAR-END

You could have an October 31st year-end if your company is on the accrual method of accounting. If your corporation makes over $250,000 net profits per year, it has to be on the accrual method of accounting. In fact, as a general rule, all "C" corporations must be on the accrual method of accounting, unless the corporation is a personal service corporation. You'll have to see your local CPA for more information on implementation and possible impacts.

> **THE ACCRUAL BASIS IS BEST**

If you are on an accrual basis of accounting, you may use the $2^1/_2$ month rule. This allows the corporation to pay out money, but the recipient doesn't have to claim it for $2^1/_2$ months. For example, a salary or bonus paid out to an employee of your corporation lets the corporation deduct it immediately, but the employee receiving it does not have to claim it for $2^1/_2$ months. Go back to October 31st: the corporation writes a check on or before October 31st in the form of bonuses, salaries, et cetera. You would not have to claim that money as income for $2^1/_2$ months, which brings you into January. This gets the money into the next year.

Other year-end angles in regard to corporations are to:

1) Control the timing of payments on bills.

2) Determine whether you want more money this year or next. Take an aggressive stance at collecting receivables. If receiving extra money is not going to hurt as badly, or if you have projects going on in the next year and anticipate making a larger amount of money, you may want to accelerate the income into the current year. You could even give cash discounts for paying early, and other strategies to build up your income or change the income from next year to this year, and likewise from this year to next year.

MOVE MONEY TO NEXT YEAR

3) If you do what I propose—use multiple corporations with different owners and different entities which own one type of a corporation, or controlling entity managing another corporation—and if you are the management corporation then one corporation can pay another corporation towards the end of the year. You could literally mail off a check to your bank account or to your corporate

headquarters in Las Vegas and have that money receipted four, five, or six days later in the mail and deposit it. So you have, in effect, one corporation deducting money at one year-end, either December 31st or January 31st, and another corporation being able to take that money out right now as income at its year beginning. For tax purposes, the money received would be claimed in the next year and the corporation would have a whole year with that money to expense it out or shelter it with other deductions.

It is pretty amazing how many checks are put in the mail on December 28th and 29th, and how many people do last minute tax shelter type purchasing in the last few days of the year just to get whatever tax breaks that they can get. I believe that we get so busy making money, so busy doing the day-to-day mundane things of running our companies, that we forget the biggest expense that we're going to have is what we owe the IRS. And this usually doesn't become apparent until April 15th. When it does, people are upset because all year long they have been haggling and negotiating over saving a few cents off of products they purchased. We spend a lot of time trying to make more money and to save money. Then we realize that what is more important than the unit costs of the products we are marketing, more important than our employee costs, and more important than the rent on our buildings, is this expense to the IRS. The irony is that we get zapped with the higher tax when we run our businesses better, and the more effective we are (we increase sales and decrease expense), the more money we owe the IRS. So the IRS becomes the beneficiary of 30 to 40% of all of our business prowess. This book should not be the end of your studies to minimize this tax bite. Study everything. Study the pertinent items for your type of business. Get an aggressive tax counselor. Go to seminars and put education on the front burner.

THE IRS GETS A LOT OUT OF OUR PROFITS

Chapter Eight

Pension Plans

"If we don't change our system of collecting taxes, it will break down...our traditional approach cannot sustain an acceptable level of compliance."

—IRS Commissioner Shirley Peterson, to the annual meeting of the New York Bar Association's tax section (January 31, 1993)

The following is a brief outline of pension planning which highlights the key areas. I started by making money in real estate and taught seminars on these methods, but as I got more deeply involved in the seminar business, I realized we were attracting a large group of people who already had their own businesses. It became a natural course of events to teach people how to save and use what they were making in a more efficient way. I want to introduce you to a way of socking aside substantial amounts of money into your own retirement account. You'll then learn how to work that money and take control of your financial destiny. There are two primary purposes for this:

> **GET READY FOR A GREAT RETIREMENT**

1) To help you see how you can put aside this "pre-tax" money, and give you more information on what you can do with it to create a secure financial future. There are obvious limitations on how much detailed information I can give here. So refer to the audio workshop, *Pension Power*, for more information.

2) You may want to set up a Pension Plan yourself. If you do, I hope you will allow our company to set it up for you.

Imagine having a tax-free investment—income with no tax liability. The only investment I can think of that truly fits the definition of a tax-free investment is a municipal bond. How would you like to have an entity that functions on its own and has its own Federal ID number, a self-contained entity which would take any and every investment you want to get involved in, and make them tax-free investments? In effect, all your investments held within this entity would become tax-free investments.

CHOOSE YOUR INVESTMENTS WISELY

I know you have heard about IRAs. You can put aside $2,000 a year, possibly $4,000 for husband and wife. The problem with IRAs is they are so limited in what they can do. You may find a bank that will fund different investments, but they are limited. They want you to purchase their line of products, such as savings accounts and CDs. And if you use an insurance company, they have different annuity-type products. Stockbrokers allow a little more flexibility, but you're still limited and exposed to commissions and their sales pitch on the "investment du jour." If you are going to fund of IRA, be sure to investigate the "Roth-IRA" which permits tax free withdrawal of both earnings and principal tax free! See your advisor.

These outfits have stocks, bonds, mutual funds, real estate investment trust units (REITS), and some have Limited Partnerships. However, you are still limited to what they have and most of those are very boring investments. They may be safe (maybe not), but they are not going to get you great returns.

DIFFERENT TYPES OF PLANS

I'm going to show you a whole different way of looking at your financial future. What I'm talking about is a qualified Corporate Pension

Plan, or for the self-employed, a KEOGH plan. Let's look at the Corporate Pension Plan. Within this designation there are basically two approaches: the Defined Benefit Plan and the Defined Contribution Plan.

I want to concentrate on the Defined Benefit plan first. In a Defined Benefit plan you define your benefit: how much you will take out of the Pension Plan upon your retirement. Now to retire you have to be $59^1/_2$ to start. At $70^1/_2$, it is mandatory. You can be older than $70^1/_2$ and still put money in the plan, but you also have to pull money out of the plan. If you start pulling out before $59^1/_2$, you have to pay the 10% penalty and taxes on the money you pull out.

> **PUT ASIDE SUBSTANTIAL AMOUNTS IN DEFINED BENEFIT PLANS**

But, let's say you are in your 30s, 40s, or 50s and you really want to put aside substantial amounts of money for a great retirement. You choose the age you want to retire, for instance age 65. Based on the money you have been making, you determine to pull out $3,000 per month. In order to pull out $3,000 per month at age 65, based on how much interest the money will be earning, and based on how much longer you will live, you determine you will need $400,000 earning interest to produce $3,000 per month for the rest of your life. You see, we have now defined the benefit.

If you are 35, you have 30 years to put in your $400,000. However, if you are 50, 52, or 59, you have only six or eight years to put aside $400,000. You can put aside substantial amounts, sometimes $60,000, $70,000 or $80,000 per year in a Defined Benefit Plan. Older people who are making really good money should look at a Defined Benefit Plan. However, Defined Benefit Plans have become very paper intensive and cumbersome the last few years. There are many people abandoning their Defined Benefit Plans for an easier, simpler Defined Contribution Plan.

In a Defined Benefit Plan, you are defining how much money you are going to pull out. In a Defined Contribution Plan, it is the direct opposite. It is based on what you are going to put in. It's a percentage of your compensation, or a percentage of the net profit of your company if it is a sole proprietorship (or S-Corporation).

Here are the numbers. In a Defined Contribution Plan there are really two sides. Generically, it is called a Pension Plan. Technically, it is either called a Money Purchase Plan, or a Profit Sharing Plan.

PUT ASIDE 1 TO 25% OF THE COMPENSATION

In the Money Purchase Plan (this is for a corporation) you can put aside from 1 to 25% of the compensation. This includes salaries, bonuses, and other things pulled out of the company by you and your employees. In the Profit Sharing Plan you can put aside from 2 to 15%. The amounts are different because the money going into a Money Purchase Plan is fixed. It's mandatory for you to put aside that amount of money every year. If this sounds scary to you, especially new businesses that are not bringing in substantial amounts of money on a regular basis, then consider the Profit Sharing Plan where the amount of money is flexible, totally discretionary.

You can change your mind every year. If you don't make a profit with your company, you don't have to put any aside. So at the end of the year you can decide what amount of money would be best, considering your profit margin or money available. If, for instance, at the end of the year, you have $6,500, you could put $3,500 in the Profit Sharing Plan. It's totally flexible.

For most small businesses, the Defined Contribution Profit Sharing Plan is what gives them the most flexibility. What I just showed you is for a corporation. And remember, for a corporation the percentage goes up to 25%. If you have a Profit Sharing Plan, the percentage goes up to 15%. Later on you could add the Money Purchase Plan side and have an additional 1 to 10% going in to reach the 25% maximum. But remember, that portion is fixed.

The corporation just can't sell off assets, acquire a bunch of money and then put it aside. It is based on money paid out to the employees of the corporation. You may be the only employee. Once it is paid, a percentage can be put aside as a donation into the Pension Plan from the corporation.

SOLE PROPRIETORSHIPS USE 'NET PROFIT'

If you have a sole proprietorship, an "S" corporation falls under this category, the maximum you can put aside is 20% of the whole net profit of the company. If you have your own business, or if you have your own sole proprietorship, do you have a regular steady paycheck or do you just take money whenever you need it? With most small businesses, if there is money in the cash register they go get it. Whether they pull it out or not, they still have to pay taxes on it! Therefore, the amount of money (0 to 20%) which can be put aside is based on the full amount of the net profit of the company.

It does not matter whether you're a corporation at 25% or a sole proprietorship at 20%. Either way you go, you can still put aside more than $20,000 per year, per person. The maximum amount the donation can be based on is $160,000. That could be $20,000 for the husband and $20,000 for the wife. Where does this money go? It goes into your own pension retirement account. You go down to a bank and set up an interest-bearing checking account. Maybe it will take $50 or $100 to open up the account. Then month after month, year after year you're able to start socking aside huge amounts of money, up to $20,000 or $40,000 or more per year. If you have employees in your controlled corporation, you're going to include all of your employees. This could be one of the greatest things for keeping your employees working for you.

And if they quit, only a portion (what has been vested to that point in time) goes to them. The balance is distributed to the accounts of the other members of the plan by their respective shares of ownership. More than likely, a substantial part of this will be distributed to you. The maximum annual contribution is $30,000 per person.

I'm going to give you an example of what this means. Let's say you have a small company and you're grossing about $200,000 a year. Your expenses are about $80,000. That leaves $120,000 net profit for your company. Let's say this is a sole proprietorship so the percentage we'll use is 20%. If you take 20% of this net profit, you would have $24,000. You take $24,000 and put it aside into this other interest-bearing checking account. This money can start earning interest from day one. It could go into a brokerage account and start earning money there by buying stocks and bonds. Because this becomes a deduction to your company, the new net profit of your company is $96,000, not $120,000. If you're in a 30% tax bracket, 30% of $24,000 is $7,200. If you don't have a Pension Plan, this $7,200 is going to the IRS.

Here's the point. You are going to write a check. You don't have a choice in that. Your choices are to write out a check to the IRS, or to write out a check to your financial future. And now, with this incredible Pension Plan, you can sock aside a huge amount of money every year and fully deduct it.

WRITE A CHECK TO YOUR FINANCIAL FUTURE

How Big?

People ask me that all the time, "How big should my company be to have its own Pension Plan? Let's look at the small numbers. If you have a small sole proprietorship and you are only making $15,000 net a year, you could have an IRA put aside $2,000. But if you take 20% of the $15,000 it would be $3,000. You could put $2,000 into an IRA or you could put $3,000 into your own pension account. Which one is better? Also, at this level of income you could not only have your own Pension Plan, you could also have an IRA on top of that. So you could put aside $3,000 into a Pension Plan and $2,000 into an IRA.

Continuing with this example, if you put $2,000 into an IRA, you are severely limited on what you can do. Yes, it can go into a brokerage account and make a few, specific investments. But if you have your own pension account and you've socked aside that $3,000, you can go out and loan money; you can get involved in start-up companies and invest in private corporations. If you like buying and selling properties, you could take that $3,000 and buy a dumpy, fixer-upper house with $2,000 down. Remember, you are the trustee. You are fully empowered with the right to take care of your own financial destiny. You take out a couple thousand dollars and put it down on a little fixer upper property, go to Ace Hardware store and buy $85 worth of paint, buy a few hundred dollars worth of carpeting, and then fix it up. After the house is fixed up, it sells for $5,000 down and $650 a month. The $5,000 goes back into the pension account and the monthly checks coming in off the note you've created also go into the pension account.

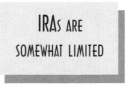

IRAS ARE SOMEWHAT LIMITED

I've seen people start with a few thousand dollars and build up hundreds of thousands of dollars in equity. One woman put aside $50,000 into her Pension Plan and for the next few years she didn't put aside anymore. But she had some good investments with her pension money and her account had grown to be worth $85,000. Her son came to her and said, "Mom I need to borrow $50,000 for a down payment on a home." Her Pension Plan loaned him the $50,000. She took a 11% second mortgage with a $650 a month payment. What a great investment for a Pension Plan—getting 11% at $650 a month! Now, think about that. Do you think she would have liked to have loaned her son that money anyway? Probably so, but this way she was

BUILD UP QUICKLY

able to take the money, sock it aside, not pay taxes on it, and have had it all available for investing. It continued to grow, and with "before tax" money she was able to help her son and help her Pension Plan at the same time.

To summarize, Defined Benefit Plans are good, especially if you are older and making really good money. The more popular one right now is called a Defined Contribution Plan (a Money Purchase and/or Profit Sharing Plan). One more thing about Defined Benefit Plans: you can only put aside so much money. Let's say at age 65 you want to retire and you need that $400,000. If along that road to making the $400,000, you get ahead of yourself and if your investments do really well, you may have to revert some of that money out of the Pension Plan and your corporation would have to claim it.

However, there is no such ruling with a Defined Contribution Plan. You file annual contributions and they grow into a huge amount of money—one, two or three million dollars. All that money will be available for disbursement upon your retirement. Defined Contribution Plans are really the best choice, particularly for those of you who are just getting started.

POPULAR PLAN— DEFINED CONTRIBUTION

What is your role? There are three people involved with the Pension Plan. One is the sponsor of the plan—that will be you and/or your company. Another will be the trustee or administrator—the person handling the money and that will be you. The last one is the beneficiary, which will also be you. Your job is to make prudent investments. If you are really good at buying second mortgages for your Pension Plan, that would be a good thing to do. If you are really good at investing in start-up companies, or know how to choose mutual funds, then that would be a good, safe, investment for your Pension Plan. Prudency here means a little bit of diversification—safe investment and/or blue chip stock investments. Your company can be very aggressive and very robust, but as the trustee of the Pension Plan money for the corporation, you need to do a good job with this money.

What does it cost to set up a Pension Plan? I've seen other companies charge nearly $5,000 to set up a Pension Plan. It shouldn't cost that much. The cost of a Pension Plan should be about $2,000. That may seem like a lot of money, but if you understand what I've written already, you can save $7,000, $8,000, or $9,000 a year by socking aside this money. $2,000 is peanuts compared to the savings. You pay for the Pension Plan one time. You continually pay for not having one.

We have discounts for students who attend or purchase our programs. They can receive substantial amounts off the pensions. One of the reasons that people use us when setting up their Pension Plan is that we make them "self-trusteed." We teach them how to set up their own accounts and how to handle all their money. No one can touch the money except them. They are the only ones who have access to the checkbook and they do all of their own investments.

Another alternative would be to choose a big brokerage house. They'll charge anywhere from $500 to $5,000 to set one up and they may give you a discount on this if you are willing to use them for all of your investments. Here's the problem: these big brokerage houses and sometimes insurance companies will charge 1, 2, or 3% for "annual asset maintenance." What do they do for that? If your Pension Plan buys stocks, they are going to get a commission and on top of the normal commissions, they usually charge your accounts a "ding" fee ($15 or $20) every time they touch your pension money. At the end of the year, after you've worked hard for the last 10 or 15 years to accumulate the $400,000 in your pension account, you'll get your statement. You'll notice 2% taken out at the bottom of the page. Two percent of $400,000 is $8,000 a year—right out of your

GET CONTROL OF YOUR MONEY

account. If you use us, we have an annual fixed fee. For that, we do all of your compliance reports, addendums, and pension tax returns. (This small fee is in the hundreds of dollars, not in the thousands of dollars). We do not charge an annual asset maintenance fee. You need to be the only one touching your money and you need to have what is called a "Self-Trusteed" Pension Plan. You can open up an account at Dean Witter, Merrill Lynch or Charles Schwab, but don't have them administer your pension funds. You be the administrator and trustee of your money. Your job is to invest in stocks, bonds, mutual funds, some forms of real estate, limited partnerships, and good, solid loans. Your job is to do the very best you can with this money.

> YOUR JOB = PRUDENT INVESTING

There are ten advantages to Pension Plans that set them head and shoulders above anything else.

1) **HIGH RETURNS**
    If you want to get rich, you have to get a high rate of return on your money— 10% minimum. About 15 to 25% should be the norm. You've got to learn how to get involved in investing and get those rates of return.

2) **LEVERAGE**
    The only way to substantially get those returns over and over again is to get better at the law of leverage. For example, taking $10,000 cash and buying a $20,000 second mortgage with a nice monthly payment coming in. That is a form of leverage. Buying $10,000 of IBM stock, borrowing back $5,000 on margin, and buying some more is a form of leverage. You've got to enhance your asset base. You've got to take what little money you have and tie up as many investments as you possibly can.

> THESE PENSION TRUSTS PRODUCE `BIG TIME´ RESULTS

3) **LIQUIDITY**

Your Pension Plan needs to be liquid, allowing you to borrow money. There are a lot of limitations on borrowing the money. You can borrow for medical purposes, for buying a home, and serious things. You have to pay it back at a fair interest rate, but think of this: imagine walking into a loan office and saying, "I'd like to get a loan for $10,000." Now you jump to the other side of the table and sit in the loan officer's chair and say, "What are you going to use for collateral?" And you hop back over the desk and say, "I want to use the vested part of my Pension Plan." You hop back over the desk as the loan officer and say, "Your loan is approved." What I just did is very serious. When you become the trustor, the trustee and the beneficiary of the same money, you are now in full and complete charge of your financial future.

> **YOU ARE THE**
> `LOAN COMMITTEE`

4) **DEDUCTIBLE**

The tax deductibility of this money, by being able to sock aside $30,000 a year and by fully deducting it, simply means all of your money is going towards investments. Right now most of you are doing your investments with after-tax money. You've already paid taxes on it and whatever you have left over goes into investments. How would you like to change all that? How would you like to have all the money going into your investments with before-tax money? With a Pension Plan, you can do that, at least up to the $30,000 a year and with a Defined Benefit Plan even more.

5) **CAPITAL GAINS**
The next thing has to do with growth and capital gains. I'll bet a lot of you have properties or other investments you have purchased over the last several years and want to sell them. If you do, you are going to get killed on capital gains. If you bought the investments with your Pension Plan, selling would incur no consequences. You can get into and get out of investments with no tax implications.

NO TAX CONSEQUENCES

6) **NO TAX**
The previous advantage has to do with the income. All of your investment becomes tax deferred. Whether it's interest income, dividend income, or other types of investment income (say from Limited Partnerships), all income made within a Pension Plan is tax free. When I say tax free, the Pension Plan will never pay taxes. Of course, when you are 42, 52, or 67 years old and you decide to pull out that money, you will have to pay taxes on it in your current tax bracket. However, the Pension Plan gets to have all this money socked aside, not pay any taxes while you're putting it aside and have that money growing and getting ready for a great retirement. How many of you wish you had heard this 15, 20 or 30 years ago? Wouldn't it have been nice to have socked aside 5, 10, or 15% of all the money you've made over the last bunch of years, deducted that money, not paid taxes on it and had that money growing for your retirement?

GET GOING NOW

7) **EASY**
The Pension Plan needs to be easy. It is easy to set up, operate, and wind down when it comes time.

8) SAFETY

The Pension Plan money is safe. Let's go back to our $400,000 example. You work really hard to sock aside $400,000 into your Pension Plan. Twenty-three thousand dollars this year, $13,000 next year and $9,000, $6,000, $600 and $6,000 again. Every year you are accumulating more and it is compounding. You're finally worth $400,000. Could you or your business be faced with some kind of financial trauma in the future? Yes, you could even end up bankrupt. How would you like all the money you've socked away into your Pension Plan to be totally safe and protected where nobody could come after it? Only an ex-spouse and the IRS under certain circumstances could have access to that money. You've socked aside all this money and nobody can ever touch it. For your information, a few years ago there was an attack on a Pension Plan and it went clear to the Supreme Court. They ruled that Pension Plan money is totally safe and no one can come after that money. This is safer than a corporation. A Pension Plan, in conjunction with a corporation, is really incredible. (Also remember, you can put aside more money faster in a corporate entity than in a sole proprietorship.)

> **PENSION PLAN MONEY IS SAFE**

9) VARIETY

The Pension Plan needs to be flexible. By this I mean it can get involved in a variety of investments. Investments will change from year to year. They'll get popular and unpopular; they'll be good, then bad. You need to be able to rock and roll with the different, exciting things going on in the investment arena. You've got the checkbook and the flexibility to move the money around. Not only is a pension account another diversified entity, but it can, in and of itself, invest in a variety of investments.

10) CONTROL

You've got the checkbook. No one else is telling you what to do with your pension money. Professional pension fund administrators make, for their clients, about a 4.2% return on the money. Can you do better than that? I think so. The different investment vehicles out there and the shopping around you can do allow your plan to take on a personality of its own. Nobody is going to be as concerned about your money as you are. You need to take control of your financial destiny, and the "Self-Trusteed" Pension Plan allows you to do that.

YOU'VE GOT THE CHECKBOOK

We have a client who put aside $30,000 one year and $20,000 the next year. Now seven years later, his pension fund has cash and CDs worth 1.9 million dollars. Could he have even made that kind of money under himself? No, because every year he would have to pay taxes. Could his corporation make that kind of money? No, every year it would have to pay taxes. The only entity that can sit there and wave at the IRS and pay no taxes is a Pension Plan. However, one of the hardest things for people to realize is that if they have a choice between themselves, their company, or their pension fund getting rich, their choice should be their pension fund. They should get some money socked aside and go to work managing that money. If they could just pull enough from their company to live on, and have all their money and time working their pension trust, they would be much further ahead.

What are we working so hard for? We are all working hard so we can get money, slow down, and retire. Then why not get rich within the pension entity? Let it be the one which takes a pretty aggressive stance at making money. A few years ago my wife and I went to Sweden, Denmark, and Norway. We took a bus from Sweden to Norway and then caught a boat and went to Copenhagen, Denmark. The North Sea was really awesome. The waters there are amazingly rough and as we rolled around the side of Denmark and into Copenhagen, there was a still, calm harbor there. Well, I think that harbor is something we all need. We all need a safe harbor, a "Copenhagen," a place to put money which is safe and protected.

I'm going to go over one last aspect of this with you. A lot of you reading have probably been involved in one of these Christmas clubs, where you put aside $25 or $50 as a payroll deduction. If you stick with it, you would probably have $625 at the end of the year (including interest). It's a forced savings plan. We all need something like this in our lives. It can be easy to make money, but it is hard to have something to show for it. With your own pension fund you'll have this money growing for your retirement, safe and protected.

You can start putting aside money almost immediately. The alternatives for you are: 1) to keep paying more every year to the IRS in taxes and have nothing to show for all of your hard years of working, or 2) start making major inroads with a plan that will help you retire healthy and wealthy.

> FORCED SAVINGS PLAN

Americans earn between $1 and $2 million during our working years of (ages 25 to 65). Why then do most people end up substantially broke, and 90% of all people have to cut down their standard of living at age 65? Why are there more 18-year-olds in this country who can write a $500 check than there are 65-year-olds who can write a $500 check? At 18 they have all of their babysitting money saved up, and then they spend the rest of their lives learning how to be dead broke at age 65. Well, I asked that question at a seminar and a little old man sitting off to the side said something kind of cute. He said, "Because they spend all of their money." Well, that's the truth. If you spend all your money, you have nothing to show for it. Here is one way you can make a difference in your financial life, have your investments do the things you want them to do, and have a lot to show for your hard years of working.

NOW YOU'LL HAVE A
GREAT RETIREMENT

401(k)

A 401(k) pension plan is one where both the employer and employee participate in a shared contribution-type plan. Normally, the employer contributes a part of the money that is paid in by the employee. It could be up to 100%, however, plans have been arranged from 5% up to 50%. The employee contribution into the plan is usually done in a paycheck reduction system.

EMPLOYER AND
EMPLOYEES PARTICIPATE
TOGETHER

The amount contributed to the plan has been reduced; the amount of income it can be based on has been lowered from $235,840 to $160,000. This amount is still quite substantial and any employee with an opportunity to participate should do so. You can contribute almost $9,000 per year of your salary, beginning in 1993, to the plan.

Once the money has been set aside, the manager or trustee of the plan takes charge of the money. However, many subsequent arrangements can be made where the employee can choose the type of investments he or she wants to invest in. Usually these monies are put into a Guaranteed Investment Contract (GIC), which are mutual funds that guarantee some kind of future payout. However, some other plans purchase the employer's stock. In a private corporation, employees can end up owning a lot of its stock, but the stock may not have a high future value. In a publicly traded company, stock can be bought (usually it is bought at a discount) and, therefore, the employee can build up quite an asset base.

Other investments could be bonds or other fixed incomes, money market funds, or any other kind of balanced funds. Now many 401(k) plans are investing in international stock funds. Another type of investment could be for the plan to invest part of this money into annuities which guarantee a certain payout in the future.

On January 1, 1994, ERISA Rule 404(C) went into effect. This makes it mandatory for the employer to offer more investment options. This ruling does not apply to 403(B) plans for employees of non profit organizations and schools. Under these new rulings, the employees 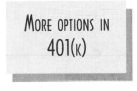 have to be given information about the different investments and be kept updated on these investments from time to time.

MORE OPTIONS IN
401(K)

The investment role of the 401(k) plan usually is tied to somebody's personality. Therefore, a very aggressive person can do an aggressive job and make or lose a lot of money depending on the types of investments. Most 401(k) plans do not, however, take a very aggressive stance. They buy a lot of stocks with growth potential, which will hopefully have some inflation hedging capabilities. In your 401(k) plan it is my recommendation that you have a diversity of investments and have a good strong asset mix.

Many people have a hard time saving money. If a 401(k) plan is made available, I advise you to take advantage of this. Because no matter what, the employer contribution could really make your assets grow a lot faster. If you're younger, we recommend that you go for high growth-type investments, and as you get in your 40s and 50s and head towards retirement, you should get a mix of those investments and equities—say 30% into fixed incomes and another 5 to 15% into international issues with high growth and some income.

ADVANTAGES FOR 401(K)

1) The income that is put into your 401(k) is not counted as income. The taxes are deferred until you draw money out. The IRS does not even withhold taxes on your 401(k) contributions.

2) Employer Matching. Over 80% of all of the plans in the United States have employers matching to some degree what the employees put in. (The most common is 50%—but it could be from 5 to 100%.)

3) 401(k) is movable. If you change jobs, you can shift your money out of a 401(k) into the 401(k) plan at your new company. Also, upon termination of your employment, you could shift the money from your 401(k) into an IRA. *[Note: if you have the money paid directly into the IRA then there is no withholding, but if you have the money paid to you and are going to take that money and put it into an IRA in the future, the previous employer will have to withhold 20% of that money. So make sure the check is not made out to you.]*

4) Most 401(k) plans have borrowing provisions so you could borrow money from the plan for emergencies. The money must be repaid within five years and you cannot deduct the interest paid on this loan.

5) For many people 401(k) is the only type of Pension Plan that their employer has, and therefore they should take advantage of this type of arrangement.

IF IT'S AVAILABLE, TAKE ADVANTAGE OF IT

Chapter Nine

Living Trusts Exposed

"American people have every right to demand a tax system they can live with."

—Former IRS Commissioner Fred Goldberg

For many years I have traveled the country teaching people how to make money, and people do make a lot of money with the information I give them. But then they have to learn to keep their money and protect their assets and all the things they have worked so hard to build up for their families upon their death. More than a decade ago I started teaching a Living Trust seminar as part of my real estate seminar. I have been well received around the country, and I have helped thousands of people set up their Living Trust. The staff I use to set up Living Trusts is second to none. They are the most competent, professional people in this country and have a great understanding of the inner workings of the Living Trust and what it really can and cannot do.

PUT YOUR FAITH IN TRUSTS

I think people have noticed a lot of ambulance-chasing attorneys teaching Living Trust seminars. It has become the new hot topic because it can be boilerplated, which means you can go into an attorney's office, he or she can fill out a little questionnaire, his secretary can go into the back room and type it up and you think you have a Living Trust. You may have the basis of a Living Trust, but if you have investments, businesses, or other assets you may not be fully protected. From this section you will have the information to understand the great attributes of a Living Trust, what it can do, and what it cannot do.

I really believe that a corporation is the greatest estate planning and asset protection tool ever designed. A simple little corporation owned by family members can do a lot to move along your estate in time of death to avoid all kinds of problems. Specifically, taxes are due upon death. Corporations are the answer to most financial problems, from a liability, lawsuit, income tax, and death tax point of view. A Living Trust needs to be used in conjunction with a corporation—not in addition to, and not because of, but in conjunction with a corporation.

THE FIVE ENTITIES

The Living Trust, Corporation, Pension Plan, Charitable Remainder Trust, and Family Limited Partnership are the five different legal entities I think you need to understand. You will then be able to see how the whole puzzle comes together. Let's talk about some of the problems associated with life. People work really hard to get money so they can slow down and retire. They start accumulating businesses, homes, other investments, stocks, bonds, mutual funds, rental real estate, notes—all kinds of investments.

FIVE ENTITIES TO
REALLY DO
THE JOB

If a person dies today, and his estate has to go through probate, that process is extensive and costly. The judge or court does not get very much money, but the attorneys that are handling the estate do get a lot of money, and unless they have pristine morals, they really have nothing at stake in ending the probate process; as long as an estate is in probate they continue to get fees. The more trouble they can cause with someone's estate, the more money they can collect. We have estates in this country that went into probate in the 1890s that are still in probate today. We have many multi-million dollar estates that went into probate in the 50s and 60s that are still open, because, if you think about it, the attorneys really have nothing at stake in ending the process. They lose their income.

WHAT IS PROBATE?

Just what is probate? If you die and you have real estate or other investments, you are not here to transfer those investments to someone else you love (like your children). The only entity besides you that can transfer your assets is a court. Probate is a legal entity set up by the government. The judge in this process will take into account all of your assets and liabilities. He will also take into account any claims on your estate, which can be from creditors or from anyone attacking your estate, such as relatives. All these different claims are validated and the judge then decides what is going to happen to your estate.

> PROTECT YOUR ESTATE

The costs associated with this are really quite awesome in that the attorneys can delve into about 10 to 20% of every estate out there. This can be a real problem because a lot of people may have just $100,000 worth of assets—and that could be their personal residence. Upon their death that whole estate has to go through probate and could cost $10 to $20,000 on just a small $100,000 estate. Therefore the probate process should be avoided.

LIVING TRUSTS VS. WILLS

The problem is that we have been taught to set up a will. We can have an attorney do it for $40 or $50 or even save money by buying a $18.95 kit and setting up the will ourselves. The problem with wills is they are an open invitation to the probate process. All wills have to be probated. So if

GET RID OF
YOUR WILL

you have a will you may want to consider getting rid of it as soon as possible and changing over to a Living Trust. A Living Trust is a separate legal entity you establish by signing documents, just like a partnership or a corporation.

Simply put, the probate process should be avoided like the plague. The average probate in America right now is $11^1/_2$ months, which can really be detrimental to your family. Guess what the number one way to avoid probate in this country is? Don't die. If you do not die, you do not have to go through probate. It's really quite simple. If you think you're going to die in the next 200 years, then the second best way to avoid probate is to not have anything in your estate. Essentially, set up another entity, a different entity away from you, and into that entity you place all of your things—including your jewelry, cars, home, investments and everything you own. This second legal entity is called a trust. The trust does not die. The trust outlives your death. So when you die, the trustee of the trust (possibly an attorney or someone you know and love whom you want to handle your estate), will settle your estate in about two hours, not $11^1/_2$ months. The cost is only a few hundred dollars, not tens of thousands of dollars and possibly hundreds of thousands of dollars, like the probate process usually costs.

WHAT LIVING TRUSTS CAN AND CANNOT DO

A TRUST IS
AN ENTITY

I want to talk about trusts in general and explain what this entity can and cannot do. There are three people involved in a trust arrangement. One is the trustor, sometimes called the settler, donor, or grantor. Essentially, the trustor is the person who establishes the trust. If you are married, the trustor will be you and your spouse. You will establish the terms of the trust, and you will determine all of the different things that will happen to the assets held in trust.

The second person involved in the trust is the trustee. The trustee is the one responsible for handling the affairs of the trust. While you are alive you will not only be the trustor (putting things into the trust), but you will be the trustee. You will be responsible for all the activities and everything that goes on in the trust, including all investments and business decisions.

> **YOU'RE THE TRUSTOR, TRUSTEE AND BENEFICIARY**

The third person involved in the trust is the beneficiary. This is the person who receives the benefits of the trust: income, assets, and disbursements of the trust. While you are living, you are the beneficiary. Upon your death, you name, or signify, who that beneficiary is going to be. It could be your children, your spouse, a charity, or anything you want it to be.

A trust document is usually 40 to 50 pages, depending on how complicated you want it. You list how many different family members you have and all your various assets. This trust becomes a legal entity. However, while you are alive it really doesn't matter how the trust was set up.

For example, if you place your personal residence into the trust, you still deduct the interest you pay on your loan for income tax purposes. If you refinance the house, you may have to take the house out of the trust just long enough to refinance. You can have loans against your property, but the property itself is placed into the trust. How do you do that? It's quite simple. You go to your title insurance company or attorney. They type up a document which usually takes 10 to 15 minutes. This is a Quit Claim Deed, or a Warranty Deed, or some such document that transfers property. It might be an assignment of contract or assignment of mortgage. You place that property, mortgage, note, or grouping of assets at Merrill Lynch or wherever you have your account. You place those assets by assigning them into the trust.

There are basically two functions of the Living Trust. The best way to understand these two functions is to see what would happen if you had only a will. If you have a will and you have jewelry, furs, cars, houses, businesses, and investments, and then you die, you, through your will, would say, "I bequeath to Johnny, my son, these things. I give to my daughter, Susan, these things." You would make a list of all the things your heirs or charities are going to receive. The same happens in a Living Trust.

After the Living Trust documents are established, one of those documents you subsequently fill out is called a schedule, which is usually referred to as a "Schedule A." On that schedule you will make a list of all your different items. The list is really split into three. You make a list of everything owned by the wife, everything owned by the husband, and everything owned by the community of the husband and wife. This list will obviously change as you go through your life. You will drop investments, you will sell jewelry, you will give away items and purchase more—things will continually change. From time to time, maybe every six months to a year, you will go in and cross off those items on the schedule that you no longer own. If you buy many other items, then you would go through and make a list of all those items. Once in a while, if there are a lot of changes on your Schedule A, you may want to go in and redo the whole thing.

YOU BEQUEATH
ITEMS SIMILAR
TO A WILL

Remember, you are the trustee. You are responsible for the affairs of the trust. You can do this by yourself, but if you need help from an attorney, we can make one available. This is really quite a simple process. You can just change the schedule by adjusting all the items in it. So the first purpose of a Living Trust is to disburse these items, similar to a will.

The second aspect of a Living Trust is far more important and far more extensive. While one aspect is to disburse items, the other aspect is to keep items together. Now think this one through. What kinds of items do you want to keep? You will probably want to keep for your family, especially if you have minor children, those items which produce income for your family—and all your investments from stocks, bonds, or real estate, and all of your investments that are producing income or are growing in value and appreciating in their capital base.

Things which you do easily may be difficult for someone else. For example, a rental property which is owned by the trust (you) may not have been a problem for you because you know how to be a good landlord, but it may be a problem for the new trustee upon your death. In your trust instructions you would say, "We want the new trustee to sell the rental and convert that money into CDs or some other investment that is easier for the new trustee to handle." But, you will want to keep a group of investments together for your future. While the trust is giving away items, a far more important function is in keeping items together under one umbrella, so one person can handle the affairs of the trust. These items you keep together could be your 30% ownership in a corporation you established with your sister. It may include other investments you have. It may include another business, any other partnership arrangements, any Limited Partnership units you own, or anything you want to keep for the future and disburse later.

THE TRUST MAKES IT EASY

The trust, because of the law of perpetuities, can only be in existence for a certain time after the death of the surviving beneficiaries. You want to make sure you control the terms of the monies being paid out, and under what terms they can be paid out. For example, if you have minor children right now and you determine upon your death that you want your children to receive money when they are 20, 25, 30, or 35 years old, you should consider not giving all the money to your children in one lump sum, but spreading it out over a period of time. You also might want them to be able to receive money if they go to college, if one of them gets sick, or if one of them wants to buy a house and needs a down payment. These are your decisions. These are the determinations you make on what you want to do with this money.

I am going to back up right now and share with you the most typical Living Trust seminar being taught all around the country. If you go to just anyone's Living Trust seminar, you will see him put $1.2 million on a screen, and say, "If you were to die, you can give to your spouse..." (He would draw an arrow to show how much you can give to your spouse.) Then he would ask, "How much can you give your wife?" People would say $600,000. The correct answer is, yes, you can give $600,000, but you can give a lot more. You can give everything to your spouse. You can give $1.2 million, you can give $10 million, you can give a billion dollars to your spouse. There are no estate taxes due upon your death if everything is given to the spouse.

However, for the 1997 tax year we have a federal exclusion of $600,000. It is a one-time "lifetime" exclusion. One time, in your life, you can give to a non-spouse $600,000. Simply put, the first $600,000 of a person's estate is not subject to estate taxes. Beginning in 1998, the exclusion increases to $625,000 to end at $1,000,000 in 2006. Even if you have used up the $600,000 in previous years, as the amount rises you can still take advantage of the higher limits. This can be given away in increments.

Are estate taxes heavy duty? Yes, they certainly are. First of all, estate taxes at one dollar over the $600,000, start at 18%, go on a graduated scale to 37%, then shoot right up to

55%. If you have a rather large estate, your family and estate are going to have to pay up to 55% of the value of all the assets you hold.

Let's go back to this other seminar. They put up $1.2 million. They pass down to the spouse $1.2 million. There are no taxes due because you can give everything to your wife. Not $600,000, but any amount you want. The wife lives for six months or six years, then passes away. The question is, how much can she give their children or their favorite charity?

When people die, how much can they give to their children or charity with no taxes due whatsoever? The answer is $600,000. They can give the whole $1.2 million to the children, but only $600,000 of their estate can go to their children without any estate taxes being due. So, $600,000 goes to the children, but that's only half of the $1.2 million. The other $600,000 that remains in the estate is now going to be subject to estate taxes. How much? On $600,000, the tax due the IRS is $235,000. People don't want to pay that kind of money. The attorney says, "Let's go back and we will do it a different way."

THE A-B TRUST

This time instead of giving all assets to the spouse directly, we are going to do it through the "A-B" format. We will not give all the assets to the spouse; instead, we will give half of the assets, or $600,000, to the spouse. How much in taxes will be due? Nothing. Because under this "A" format of the Living Trust, everything can go to the spouse and no taxes will be due. Under the "B" format, we're going to give the other $600,000, or the other half of the $1.2 million to the children. How much is due in taxes? Nothing. You can "give away" $600,000 to your kids.

TWO CHANNELS FOR THE MONEY

If you have older children, you can give half to your spouse and half to your children. You don't need a trust—you don't need anything. You just need to make arrangements to do just that. There are absolutely no taxes due, whatsoever. The problem is, what if you want to keep your estate together?

For example, what if you have minor children, or younger grandchildren you want to provide for? Then you need the "B" format to become a trust. The "B" format is called the "B Trust." We will place into this trust the other $600,000 worth of assets, money, or whatever else you own. So one amount of $600,000 goes to the spouse and the remaining $600,000 goes to the children, but through a trust. We can control the terms of this trust, under what conditions they will get the money, and in what time frame they will get the money. We are basically in control of our money, even when we are dead and gone. This is called the A-B Trust. What I think you need, especially if you have minor children, is called the ABQD Trust. "Q" stands for QTIP. Some of you might have seen articles in magazines that talk about a "QTIP Trust." They are trusts with QTIP provision means. QTIP stands for "Qualified Terminable Interest Property," and QTIP equals income.

> **QTIP PROVISIONS FOR SUPPORTING THE FAMILY**

You put aside $600,000 for your children—your spouse may not need that $600,000. What does your spouse need from that $600,000 to support the family? The answer is the income. While you put your investments away for your children, the "Q" provision and trust documents give the spouse the right to receive the income from those assets to support the family.

The "D" in ABQD stands for disclaimer. What if the spouse doesn't want the money? What if she wants half of it this year, but none of it the next year, and all of it the year after that? Maybe by receiving the money, it would throw her into a higher tax bracket, so she wants to leave the money in the trust. The "D" allows her to disclaim any or all of the money in any year she chooses. A lot of the attorneys right now, for the sake of simplicity, are calling this "Q" and "D" provision a "C" provision, or an ABC Trust. This basically establishes the trust documents, allowing the spouse to receive the income she needs to support the family.

MAKE YOUR MONEY DO MORE

However, here is another interesting point on the $600,000 one-time exclusion. Let's say you and your wife are in your early fifties. You set up a life insurance trust and gift in $600,000. The trust buys a "second to die" policy. It grows in value, and according to your actual life expectancy, it will protect over $7,000,000 in wealth—over twelve times the original amount. All of this passes to your family easily with no taxes. And for younger couples, or couples not having the ability to gift away $600,000, this same procedure works by using the annual $10,000 to $20,000 gifts. *[Note: second to die life insurance is less expensive than other life insurance, but you may not withdraw funds.]*

If you go to a seminar and say, "What if I am worth $1.4 million, or $2 or $3 million?" most of the attorneys do not have the answer. I'm not going to cover this in detail right now, but if you're worth substantially more than $1.2 million, say up to $3.2 million, then what you need is a GST or Generation Skipping Trust. Simply put, a Generation Skipping Trust allows you, as a husband and wife, to give $1 million to your grandchildren. While your children are still alive, they can live off the income from the million dollars held in trust for your grandchildren. You're skipping a generation, hence the name Generation Skipping Trust. If you need more help on this, see your attorney, or see our attorneys and we will help you get a Generation Skipping Trust established. If you think about it, everything over $3.2 million in your estate is going to be taxed and you ought to be very concerned about estate taxes.

THE GST

One of the other situations we haven't addressed yet is if you are worth a lot of money or you plan to be worth a lot of money in the future. How do you avoid these other estate taxes? The answer is easy. Just don't own those items. One of the things I love to do is set up corporations for controlling your businesses and give Mom and Dad very little of the stock. Give the parents voting stock, give the kids non-voting stock, or bigger shares of the corporation. As the stock becomes worth something, it is not in the parents' estate.

USE DIFFERENT ENTITIES

You could have a $10 million corporation. If you own 1% of that, you own $100,000 you could give away (remember you can give away up to $600,000.) By owning a corporation, you can control investments, real estate, and businesses. You don't own them, the corporations own them and your children own the bulk of the corporations. Upon your death, there is no transfer of assets, therefore, there is no transfer tax (sometimes called an estate tax).

I really love corporations in conjunction with trusts because you can have $20 or $30 million in assets and pay nothing in estate taxes. In order to move on and show you how good a trust really is, we need to define some terms. When you set up your trust, there are some other documents you need to establish, up to 18 in all.

DURABLE POWER OF ATTORNEY

One is called a "Power of Attorney." For example, I want Bill to act in my behalf if something happens to me. Bill would handle some financial matters of my estate, and I want him to buy the groceries and take care of my children. I could give Bill a Power of Attorney. How does the Power of Attorney end? We can revoke it or it ends upon incapacitation or death of one of the two people involved. The Power of Attorney ended at the time I need someone to act in my behalf.

Here is another scenario. I ask George to handle my businesses and all my investment affairs. I give him a Power of Attorney. However, I get in a car accident and I'm hospitalized in a coma for six months. That Power of Attorney is not valid if you are incapacitated. What you need is called a "Durable" Power of Attorney. It is a document that takes effect upon your incapacitation or death.

Another term that needs to be understood is "fully funded." If you set up a trust, one is funded, one is unfunded. You put assets into a funded trust and nothing into an unfunded trust. An irrevocable life insurance trust, which I really recommend if you own your life insurance policy, is an unfunded trust until you die. The trust owns the life insurance policy and upon your death, the money goes into the trust and it becomes funded at that point. Whatever you want done with the money happens at that point in time.

MAKE IT FULLY FUNDED

Fully funded has an additional aspect. We're talking about putting all the assets you own into a Living Trust. A Living Trust does not become a thing. A Living Trust becomes a way of life. You cannot be operating as an individual and as a Living Trust. You have, in a sense, ceased to exist and the Living Trust has to take over all the affairs of your life. I know that sounds weird, but that's the best way to put it.

POUR OVER WILL

The next term to learn is "Pour Over Will." It is usually one page long with notary endorsements on the back establishing that anything which has not been put into the trust will be poured into the trust upon your death. For example, if you put your home and business into the trust and acquire more items through life and forget to put those into your trust, upon your death everything that is not in your trust is poured into the trust at that time.

Another document that could be part of your Living Trust is a "Living Will." If something happens and you become incapacitated, you could determine your own fate. This includes decisions about life support systems, et cetera.

There are three major aspects of the Living Trust. Graphically, in your mind, draw a box and write Living Trust. Into this box we are going to place several items by assignment, or by deed. I believe that your personal residence should be in a Living Trust. I believe, even though a Living Trust does not afford any liability protection, it is enough protection and is the best place to put your personal residence. A Living Trust's primary function is to avoid probate. If you or your business were sued, the Living Trust affords no lawsuit protection.

Let's say, you put into your Living Trust your savings, rental properties, a sole proprietorship, and your residence. As you go through life, you end up owning 30% of a business with your sister. You buy some mortgages but you forget to put them into the Living Trust. Is this a fully-funded Living Trust? No, because you have not put those items into the trust. You have that original batch of items, but you didn't assign those other items.

Upon your death, all of the items you have put into the Living Trust avoid probate. There is a short settlement and a small fee. Every item not put in your Living Trust has to go through probate. The Pour Over Will is a simple document that assigns everything that wasn't in your trust and puts it in your trust, upon your death. Anything that was not placed in your Living Trust upon your death has to go through probate.

ARE YOU PROTECTED?

You need to make sure the Living Trust is fully-funded. You need to think about you as a Living Trust. It will buy your home, car, et cetera. If that little sole proprietorship you set up has made you money over the years, and someone comes in, falls down, sues, and gets a large judgment against you, the insurance will only pay so much. The question is, "Are you protected?" You may think your house is protected because it is in the Living Trust. However, when the "victim" gets the judgment against you, you can have liens placed against your home, rental properties, et cetera. There is no liability protection.

Therefore, you need to make sure you don't have a sole proprietorship. It's easy for income tax purposes—filing a simple return, however, a sole proprietorship is dangerous because if you are sued you can lose almost everything you own.

A corporation can protect you against these things. Your corporation becomes a separate, legal, stand-alone entity. If your corporation owns a dry cleaning business, it should not own interest in a restaurant, because everything owned by any one entity can be affected by a judgment. You may need four or five different forms of ownerships to protect all your assets. By avoiding sole proprietorships and having a corporation, you set up a legal entity called a "sponge" entity. It can soak in a lot, but nothing comes back out. So, if a corporation gets sued and loses a lawsuit, it does not go against your personal residence. The corporation has "absorbed" everything.

The next item should get you excited. Joint tenancy is a problem as we go through life. Many people don't realize this. When you buy a home, you can take joint tenancy, or tenants in common. Most professionals will tell you everyone takes joint tenancy with rights of survivorship because the husband will own 100% of the home and the wife will also own 100%. If you were to die, the other owns the house. It's an easy way to pass it on to a spouse.

From a technical point of view, there is probably nothing better than joint tenancy, but it's dangerous. In many cases it's the worst possible thing to do. Tenants in common, for protecting your personal affairs, is when the husband owns

JOINT TENANCY CAN BE DANGEROUS

50% and the wife owns 50% of the house. Upon the death of one of the spouses, they could give to the other their 50%, or it could go to their estate or to their children or grandchildren. If you die with a grouping of assets and you didn't state under what format you took title to it, a judge will rule tenants in common. A judge would act in the person's own best interest.

To show you how good a Living Trust really is, let's compare joint tenancy ownership of a home and a house deeded to a Living Trust. Let's say you bought a house many years ago for $100,000 and you took title as joint tenants. The house is now worth $500,000. The husband dies. The wife wants to sell the property. She puts the house up for sale and gets her sale price—$500,000. She receives her check.

How does the IRS treat this from a tax viewpoint? They want to calculate the capital gains. They basically take a line and draw it down the property, saying half is owned by the husband and half by the wife. The original basis was $100,000, so the wife's basis is half, or $50,000 in the property. She can inherit her husbands basis at a "stepped up" basis. This means, it is "stepped up" to the current value, in this case $500,000. The wife's half would be $250,000. Her basis in the property is $50,000. She also inherits her husband's "stepped-up" basis. So her total basis in the property is now $300,000. She has capital gains of $200,000. She must pay capital gains tax on $75,000 (or $20,000).

In this next example, we are going to own the house as a Living Trust and see what happens. When you set up your Living Trust you can deed or assign the house into the trust. The house again is worth $500,000. Once again, the husband dies and the wife sells the home for $500,000. The IRS now says the surviving spouse inherits the house at the full "stepped-up" basis or $500,000. The surviving spouse sells the home for $500,000. We subtract the basis of $500,000 and the surviving spouse has no capital gains tax to pay.

STEPPED UP
BASIS

If you have rental real estate, stocks, bonds, or a business worth a lot, and if the husband and wife have a Fully Funded Trust, every item they own is placed into the Living Trust upon the death of one of the spouses. Everything goes to the "stepped up" basis. When the husband or wife liquidates those investments, there are no capital gains to pay if they have been owned in the Living Trust. It is not just for personal residence, but for all of your investments.

Let me give you three choices on what you can do with this information:

1) You can do nothing,

2) You can get more education (through seminars, et cetera), or

3) You can set up a Living Trust.

Chapter Ten

Transferring And Controlling

"As a citizen, you have an obligation to the country's tax system, but you also have an obligation to yourself to know your rights under the law and possible tax deductions. And to claim every one of them."

–Donald Alexander, former Commissioner of the Internal Revenue Service, under three presidents.

Sometimes the best way to explain what an entity is, is to explain what it accomplishes. Other times, you define the effectiveness of a certain legal entity by explaining its relationship to other entities. And at other times you explain what an entity is by explaining what problems it solves. The latter will be the format we will take with the Family Limited Partnership. Before I discuss the Family Limited Partnership, let me explain gifting. This may seem like a strange way of starting a discussion about an entity, which has many far-reaching effects, but when I finish this discussion, you will see how it all ties together.

Gifting

One of the easiest things to talk about, yet one of the hardest things to implement, is the idea of being able to gift away things to other people and have no tax consequences. The first $10,000 of assets, investments, money, or whatever you gift to someone in any given tax year

> **Gift away $10,000 per year**

has no tax consequences either to the giver or the receiver. In most cases, the $10,000, if it were in the form of cash, would have been previously taxed to the person giving it away.

You can also give away an appreciated asset. For example, real estate or stocks you are holding can be given to a child or grandchild. The stock you bought at $1,000, could now be worth $10,000. Both the mother and the father can gift up to $10,000 annually. Therefore, if they had three children, could give away up to $60,000 (the mother plus the father, which is two, times three children, times $10,000).

START INVESTING FOR YOUR CHILDREN

Gifting is usually an issue for people who are in their older years. They realize they are going to have a substantial net worth and, therefore, a taxable estate upon their death. Five or ten years before they die, they start giving away huge amounts of assets so they can lessen the tax bite which their estate would have to pay upon their death.

If you have minor children, under the Uniform Gift to Minors Act, you could give away the $10,000 and substantially control the investment. You would have to ask your own estate and financial planning professionals to see if this is the format or method you should use.

There are a few things I would like to mention about this important topic.

DO MORE WITH THE $10,000

1) Why not give away the $10,000 in a manner in which it will eventually pay a bigger sum? Specifically, I'm talking about using the $10,000 to buy something that would be worth substantially more, either in the future or upon your death. Here are two examples:

a) A life insurance policy. Your age and health determine the size of the insurance policy you can buy. You could take a $10,000 draw and buy a paid up policy or a single premium policy. Let's say you could buy $220,000 of paid up life insurance for your $10,000, and if you're 52 years old, upon your death, whoever is the beneficiary will receive the $220,000.

b) Bonds. You could take $10,000 and buy some bonds at 8¢, 10¢, 15¢, or 20¢ on the dollar. These are discounted, zero coupon United States Treasury Bonds. Bonds vary in price from day to day. I've purchased them at 8¢ on the dollar. You can purchase the same bonds in a few months at 18¢ on the dollar, but if you are buying bonds at 10¢ on the dollar, depending on the condition of the bonds, you could buy a $100,000 zero coupon bond with a maturity in the 25 to 30-year range for $10,000. Instead of giving away $10,000, why not give away a $100,000 bond that costs $10,000? You know at some point in time the recipient of this bond, if he holds it to maturity, will have the entire $100,000.

2) I see three problems with gifting:

a) The number one problem with gifting is that most people do not have nice, neat, little chunks of $10,000 investments laying around the house. They may have $80,000 equity in a rental

GIFTING IS DIFFICULT TO DO

property but how do you give away $10,000 worth of $80,000 equity? You may have a $10,000 CD, but you probably don't have two $10,000 CD's. The problem is coming up with gifts that are easy to give away.

b) The second problem is that gifting may trigger a property tax increase if you were to give away your property. This usually does not happen, but it could.

c) Problem number three, and this is the biggest problem: once you have given away all of your things, and it is time for your retirement years, you want to live well and have a great retirement—but all your assets are gone. You have given away everything.

The question is, "How can you give away this $10,000 a year to lessen your estate tax liability and also provide for your loved ones, in nice, neat groupings of money, having them so they trigger no tax increases, and having everything so you still control it and can live on it while you are alive?" The simple, best answer to this is a Family Limited Partnership.

The problems I just mentioned are the reasons why you will see them getting more and more popular. They are, for those of you who have existing assets, one of the easiest ways to gift things away and still control them.

GIVE AND YET MAINTAIN CONTROL

Remember, the general partner (you and your spouse) controls the investments. You control the direction of the company, the money paid out, any investment the company will buy, and any monies placed into a Pension Plan. You control everything. You could put into a partnership all of your assets and all of your investments and stocks owned from different corporations. (These could be your own small family corporations.) All of these could be owned or controlled by a Family Limited Partnership.

A partnership has units (i.e. 10,000 units, 50,000 units, 100,000 units). Remember the limited partners (you and your children) have limited liability. You would give the children very few units at first, because you don't want to trigger any tax consequences. Mom and Dad, in effect, own all the units at the start. Then, year after year, as a book entry, you would gift away some of the units. Mom and Dad are the general partners so they still maintain control, but the limited partners at first are the parents, and subsequently will be the children, grandchildren, nieces, nephews, churches, charities, or anybody else to whom you would want to gift those units. Upon your death, you have a substantially smaller estate and at the same time, you control all of these investments and all of the income they generate so you can have a great retirement.

FAMILY LIMITED PARTNERSHIPS

Limited Partnerships, or more specifically Family Limited Partnerships, are becoming the "buzz" word on the lecture circuit today. I see attorneys teaching about these new Living Trust seminars everywhere I go. Living Trusts are wonderful, but they are also very limited. They do not protect you against lawsuits. They are unable to gift or control the day-to-day workings of assets in an estate (especially if you have multiple businesses, different enterprises, and investments that are quite cumbersome.) A Living Trust is not the sole answer. It can become part of a complete estate planning vehicle when used in conjunction with corporations and Family Limited Partnerships. An increasing amount of attorneys are now realizing the limitations of a Living Trust. At first, all they taught was that a Living

> USE A FAMILY LIMITED PARTNERSHIP

Trust was a panacea for everything. Now they realize they need another entity, and without realizing the full workings of the corporation, they turn to the Family Limited Partnership.

Most people know that a corporation can cost anywhere from a few hundred dollars (if you set up one yourself) up to a few thousand dollars. Please do not set up a corporation yourself unless you have the legal expertise to determine the par value of the stock; how much stock to issue; the different types of stock and voting rights; and all the different parts that go into making it legitimate—not only with the state but with other government entities. However, with the Family Limited Partnerships, attorneys could easily charge $2,500 to $8,000. Partnerships should not cost that much to set up.

ENTITIES HAVE SPECIFIC ROLES

Before I talk about setting one up, I want to talk about why they are needed. I really believe that Family Limited Partnerships have a specific role in family investment and business situations. They specifically have a role for those people that already have substantial assets, whether those assets are held directly under themselves, in joint tenancy between husband and wife, or in the name of a corporation. An all-encompassing Family Limited Partnership can really bring diversity, power, and dynamics to your estate planning situation.

Let's say, for example, you have accumulated about $2 million worth of assets. If you were to die, $1,000,000 of your estate is not taxed under the current tax law. The other $1 million is going to be taxed. This means at the time of your death, within a short period of time, someone from your estate is going to have to come up with $435,000, and the IRS wants "cash," not assets. This could be a real hindrance to your estate after you are gone.

Simply put, there is no one who will work as hard to keep your estate together as you worked to build it up. Imagine having all you have worked for your whole life being controlled by government officials. A Living Trust can provide for the continuity of your investments and businesses in a safe way; however, a Living Trust is not the only thing you need.

WHO WILL KEEP YOUR ESTATE TOGETHER?

A Family Limited Partnership is simply a "limited partnership" with the idea that only family members are to be involved—such as children, nieces, nephews, grandchildren, sometimes friends or business partners.

A Limited Partnership is a legal entity established by a group of documents which in turn establish a purpose for the business "to be in business." It identifies the nature of the business and who the owners of the business are. The partnership has its own Federal ID number and it takes on an identity of its own similar to a trust or corporation. It is a separate, legal, distinct entity. It has its own liability protection aspects; it can buy and sell things; it can conduct business; it can own stock in corporations; it can have its own brokerage account; and it can own a lot of your personal family assets that you might have a hard time dividing up. The partnership can own everything and the units of the partnership can be owned by different people. If you have a high degree of vulnerability to lawsuits, you may also want to have your personal residence placed into a Limited Partnership.

THE FLP CAN DO A LOT OF THINGS

The word limited means "limited liability," but it does not mean limited voting rights or limited numbers of people. Limited liability means the limited partners can only lose the amount of their individual investment. Let's say ten of us get together and decide to buy an apartment complex, and I'm the general partner. Each of the ten limited partners puts up $10,000. We buy this building together and I forget to get insurance. The building burns down and we lose millions of dollars. Each of the ten limited partners could only lose

$10,000 because of the limit in liability. I, however, am the general partner. I don't have limited liability. I am liable for all the activities of the partnership.

Even though I have made being a general partner look bad, you still need to be the general partner. You need to be in control of all your family's investments and businesses. You need to control the checkbook and direction of the company, the investments you're getting into and out of, and which businesses you're buying and selling.

YOU NEED TO BE THE GENERAL PARTNER

You need to control all of your stock ownership and the voting rights of the stocks you own. You need to control what is going to be put into a pension account for you. In short, you need to control everything. The person that controls everything is the general partner. Limited partners have no say in the running of the partnership.

Partnerships can solve one of the greatest tax problems by lessening your estate. I have discussed gifting—where you can give away $10,000 a year per child/parent and not have any tax consequences. This is income you have already possibly paid taxes on, or investments that may have grown in value. As you gift it to your child there are no tax consequences.

In a corporation, ownership is called stock or shares of the company. In a partnership, ownership is called units. People who own units are called unit holders. Let's say, for example, that you set up a partnership with 100,000 units and were to give a substantial number of those units to your children at the very beginning. If those units are worth a lot of money, then you would have a problem with the gifting rules. Remember, only $10,000 a year can be gifted with no tax consequences. If, however, when you first set up this partnership, the mother and father keep the bulk of the units in their own names (50% to the mother and 50% to the father—of 100,000 units), each one of the parents would

UNITS FOR GIFTING

own 50,000 units and the children would own none. The parents may then gift to each child $10,000 worth of units each year.

You can assign, deed, transfer, or place into it everything you own of a financial nature: investments, stocks, bonds, real estate, limited partnership units in public or private partnerships, your corporation stocks in publicly traded companies, and even the corporation stock you personally own in your family corporations. Now the partnership is worth a few million dollars. The partnership takes control of all those assets and has its own checking account. It is paying the bills, receives monies and is operating similar to any other business.

Remember, the partnership is a separate legal entity—it has its own Federal ID number. It has been recorded with the county, so you can transfer real estate—any title company can help you do this. By the way, I have never seen a case wherein the parents transferred their properties into the Limited Partnership and their property taxes increased. Technically it could happen, but I've never seen it. I'll give you an example: Mom and Dad's three children own 0% of the units. Mom owns 50,000 units and Dad owns 50,000 units. Let's figure out what each unit is worth. There are 100,000 units spread between Mom and Dad. Therefore, they own all of the units in the partnership. They would divide the units into the net worth of the company. If all the equities on the properties, investments, and businesses total $2 million, then each unit is worth $20. At the end of the year (December 31st), they determine a value of the holdings of the partnership. With each unit worth $20, the mother gifts to the children enough units to equal $10,000. They don't receive any of the assets or cash; they receive units. Now instead of

DETERMINE THE VALUE EACH YEAR

Mom owning the 50,000, she owns 50,000 minus 500 each for her three children (1,500) or 48,500. They can give away all their units this year if they want to, but that would mean some heavy-duty tax consequences. If they want to stay within the law and avoid that, they would do so by using this format of giving the amount of units away that equal the $10,000. The general partners must keep 1% of the Limited Partnership units.

TAX CONSEQUENCES

Partnerships of this sort are not taxed at the partnership level. Each year, the profits or losses are calculated and passed down to the tax brackets of the respective unit holders. For example, if you own 20% of the units in a partnership, you would be taxed on 20% of the profits.

People get involved in partnerships and don't realize they will be taxed on money whether the money is pulled out or not. The general partners could decide not to disburse any funds at the end of the year to the limited partners. Even though the limited partners did not receive any of the money they made, they would still be taxed and this could be quite a tax bite around April 15th.

TAX AT THE OWNER'S TAX RATES

Conversely, if the partnership loses money, the losses would pass down to the individual tax brackets of the unit holders. Look at the following diagram and see how to set up a partnership of three children and two parents:

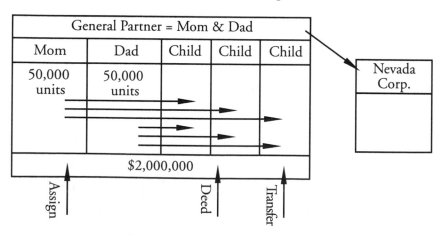

$2,000,000 Investments

You can see by looking at this diagram the partnership owns all of the different investments that were previously owned by you. *[Note: if you study other sections of this book, you'll realize that I firmly believe your assets should be split up. For the sake of simplicity, we are going to leave the $2 million in one Limited Partnership. In reality, if you were worth $2 million, this should be set up in five, six, or seven different partnerships and two or three corporations for owning and controlling that much in assets. But again, it would be hard to see how this works from a multiple point of view if you don't see how this works from a single entity point of view.]*

Your children, at first, own none of the units, but now we are going to give them some of the units. This could be done by giving them a certificate each year, but it is usually done by a journal entry in the back of your partnership documents. At the end of the year you could transfer the number of units that would equal the $10,000 (if you're trying to avoid taxation) and give that many units away.

In our example, we have 100,000 units. The partnership is now worth $2 million, so each unit is worth $20. You would give each of your children 500 units per parent. This would effectively transfer $10,000 per child (three children times two parents equals $60,000 a year). It would still take many years to get your $2 million estate down under $600,000 so that there is no tax at all.

Let me reiterate here—the partnership is not taxed. The tax is to the individual unit holders. If you have a $100,000 to $200,000 plus business and your children end up owning the bulk of the units as in the diagram below, one thing the business has going for it is excess cash flow and an opportunity to get the money into different tax brackets.

LOSSES PASS DOWN TO INDIVIDUAL TAX BRACKETS

The following diagram is for people who do not have assets and who are just starting out or have an existing business that is making a lot of money but do not have many assets.

General Partner = Nevada Corporation which Mom and Dad control				
Mom	Dad	Child	Child	Child
5,000	5,000	30,000 units	30,000 units	30,000 units

Originally 50,000

GIFT UNITS TO CHILDREN

You can see in the diagram the children own 30% each, or have 30% of the $200,000 of income, which is $60,000, in their tax bracket. The parents' percentage is kept small and their income from other sources keeps them in a 15% tax bracket. All this money taxed to the family would be taxed at 15%, not at 28, 31, or 36%.

Let's see what happens after a few years when the units have been transferred to the children. Look at the following diagram:

General Partners				
Mom	Dad	Child	Child	Child
20,000	20,000	20,000 units	20,000 units	20,000 units
$2,000,000				

You can see the children now own substantial numbers of units, but even though ownership of the Limited Partnership units has changed, the general partners are still in control of the cash flow direction and pension planning of the partnership.

Also note, the partnership buys and sells the properties, investments, and runs this grouping of investments just like any other company or individual would do with its financial affairs.

PARENTS STILL CONTROL

Another important aspect to the Family Limited Partnership is the layer of liability and lawsuit protection. As your family gets older, the children could get into their own financial situations and cause some problems. You may have built up some substantial assets for your children and one lawsuit could cause a situation where people start coming after their assets. If they have corporate stock, it can be attacked and even taken away. If they have other kinds of investments held in their personal names, those could also be taken away from them. In the Federal Partnership Act, units in a Limited Partnership can not be deprived from people.

To illustrate this point, let's say your children end up with 20,000 units and each one of those units is worth $20. Twenty thousand units times $20 is $400,000. One of your children has a lawsuit against him for $100,000, and the person suing tries to take away his units. They cannot do so, but they can get a "charging order" against the units. Then at the end of the year, the general partner chooses not to disburse any funds on the Limited Partnership units. The partner chooses, instead, to pay out more fees to the general partners whose entity could pay out money in different ways. Nevertheless, the money is withheld.

Let's say the amount of money attributed to those 20,000 units is $5 each, or $100,000. The general partner, by withholding income, creates a situation where the money is not disbursed, the Limited Partner still has to claim the money as

UNITS ARE PROTECTED

income. The person who has sued your children would have to claim $100,000 of income and pay taxes on that even though they did not receive any money (due to a charging order against the income). You can see they'll cancel the charging order really fast. Anybody in their right mind who has a lien or judgment against any of the limited partners will not attach this charging order to the Limited Partnership units because of the potential tax situation.

Another important point: when you set up your Limited Partnership, make sure the general partner is your Nevada corporation. Think about what this does—you avoid all personal liability. The corporation can be the general partner. The corporation can receive fees for doing so. The corporation can be owned by people other than those involved in the Limited Partnership, and it could be owned by the same people in different percentages. This is also one way of moving money from one state to another. A partnership in one state can pay fees to a general partner in another state for managing its affairs.

This is what we've accomplished with a partnership: we've avoided all personal liability, created a better tax situation, created another level of liability protection, and given ourselves the ability to move money from one entity and one tax jurisdiction to another. All in all, the Family Limited Partnership is a tremendous vehicle for accumulating wealth, controlling wealth, and passing the wealth along.

CAN'T TAKE AWAY ANY UNITS

In regards to gifting, I have already isolated three main reasons why people do not use the gifting laws to the fullest extent: problem #1 is grouping assets; problem #2 is incurring any type of property tax increases; and problem #3 is having all of your assets depleted from gifting them all away. By setting up a Family Limited Partnership, this one legal entity solves all three problems:

1) We now have nice groupings of money. Each year we can figure out what the units are worth. Either by our best guess estimation or by an actual appraisal on the different investments and then gift away the amount that equals exactly the $10,000. We are gifting away units in a partnership and the partnership still owns the different investments.

2) I've never seen a case in which transferring things into partnerships has increased property taxes.

3) Even though a substantial part or even all of the partnership units have been gifted, the general partners (you as a husband and wife) through your Nevada corporation, are still in control of everything.

We now have the best of all worlds. We've remedied the problems of ownership, control and cash flow.

THIS PARTNERSHIP HAS ACCOMPLISHED A LOT

It is somewhat unfair to make the following comparison. The corporation and the Limited Partnership have so many positive attributes. They are the workhorses of any business structure. Many people wonder which is the best, so I've decided to write this comparison. My fear is that people will think one is better than the other. Nothing could be further from the truth. There is no good, better, best. There are, however, different functions for each. In some cases, the two may be interchangeable. In other cases, one would be preferable over the other. This chart will help illustrate the differences.

FAMILY LIMITED PARTNERSHIP: A COMPARISON WITH CORPORATIONS

ITEM	CORPORATION	LIMITED PARTNERSHIP
SET UP	Articles formed and recorded at state level. Record (copies of articles) of filing necessary for transactions: opening a bank account, buying property.	Agreement drafted and signed by Limited Partnership memorandum or affidavit of partnership filed with state; (some) filed in county for real estate transactions.
CONTROL	Voting shareholders elect directors on annual basis. Directors choose/appoint officers: President, Vice President(s), Secretary, Treasurer. Management could be others, but usually day-to-day operations are handled by officers.	General partner selected to conduct all partnership affairs. Could be co-general partners, i.e., husband and wife. General Partner could be corporation—see section on selecting a Nevada Corporation as General Partner
DURATION	Perpetual. Could be in business hundreds of years.	Has a set time for its existence; usually one to ten years. Could be ten to twenty years. Could terminate on death of partners.

ITEM	CORPORATION	LIMITED PARTNERSHIP
MISSION	Could be varied and can change as time goes on.	Usually has definite purpose, i.e. own a building, run a business, et cetera.
LIABILITY (Investors)	No liability for corporation activities, debts, et cetera. Only amount investor could lose would be his/her invested amount.	Limited partners have "limited" liability. Limited partners can only lose what they have invested.
LIABILITY (Management)	Officers not liable for corporate activities or debt unless they do something illegal.	General Partner(s) could be liable for all partnership activities. [Note: this is the reason for a Nevada Corporation.]
EASE OF SET UP	Very cost efficient. Can be done in a few days.	Same.
ANNUAL FEES	From $75 to $300 to keep corporation active.	No fees in most states. However, Some charge a small "Franchise Fee."

ITEM	CORPORATION	LIMITED PARTNERSHIP
TAXES	(a) Has its own tax brackets. Smaller taxes paid than for sole proprietorship.	(a) Income is taxed to Limited Partners based on their respective shares of ownership.
	(b) Most avoid income pay outs. No dividends to eliminate double taxation of income.	(b) No double taxation—all income and losses attributed to Limited Partners. Income is taxed to partners even if not received by partners.
	(c) Can pay out and deduct bonuses.	(c) Can pay out and deduct salary and bonuses.
	(d) Can have off year-end, i.e. Jan. 31, Mar. 31. Can have a short year.	(d) Year-end must be same as Limited Partners, usually Dec. 31.
	(e) Losses held at corporation level. If "S" election is made, partners' losses pass through to shareholders.	(e) Unit pay out is unearned income (no Social Security due).
	(f) Can take advantage of many tax shelter strategies and vehicles.	(f) Same.
	(g) Salary, bonus treated as earned income—taxes due but are deductible to the corporation.	

ITEM	CORPORATION	LIMITED PARTNERSHIP
OWNERSHIP	Stock can be owned by any entity. Personal, different corporation, pension trust, et cetera. [*Note: "S" Corporation stock may only be owned by individuals and certain trusts, i.e. living*].	Units can be owned by those same entities.
PENSION PLANS	Wide range of programs available. Corporate pension and profit-sharing plan, 401(k) et cetera.	Treated like sole proprietorships— KEOGH. Still can put aside substantial sums of money.
GIFTING	Owners can gift away up to $10,000 worth of stock to others without tax consequences.	Owners can gift units in the same way.
PLACEMENT OF ASSETS	Deeding items to corporation trigger sale (therefore capital gains) to you. Rule 351 eliminates this if properly done.	No sale of deeded items triggered by contributing assets to the partnership.
ESTATE PLANNING	Great if used properly. (a) Can have different classes of stock.	Same. (a) Only one type of units—limited liability.

ITEM	CORPORATION	LIMITED PARTNERSHIP
ESTATE PLANNING (continued)	(b) Can have voting and non-voting.	(b) No voting rights; General Partner controls everything.
	(c) Can gift stock to redeem.	(c) No.
	(d) Can donate stock to Charitable Remainder Trust.	(d) Can gift units to redeem estate.
		(e) Same with units.
DAY-TO-DAY USE	Easy to operate because it is well accepted.	Easily recognizable but not as well accepted for business endeavors.

In summary, when in doubt, set up a corporation. Limited Partnerships are good for people who already have acquired substantial wealth and want to give it away yet still use and control it. I also think Limited Partnerships are valuable for tax planning (high cash-flow business/rentals/other). The corporation is used for owning business, real estate, other stock, and family investments for ease of use and structuring.

Chapter Eleven

Put Your Faith In Trusts

"When Congress talks of tax reform, grab your wallet and run for cover."

–Senator Steve Symms, Idaho

The main concept behind the formation of trusts is to put things such as investments, properties, and rights (right to vote, copyrights, et cetera) under the control of someone else for the benefit of a third party. The three people that are involved in the trust formation are the trustor, the trustee, and the beneficiary. The trustor, which is also the grantor, the settler, and the donor, is the person who sets up the trust and puts the asset, investment, or money into the trust. The trustee is the person responsible for handling the affairs of the trust. The beneficiary is the person who will receive the benefit later on. This could be income or some other benefit.

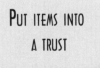

Put items into a trust

Trust law has become very sophisticated. For example, people holding beneficial interest could have something akin to voting rights and control the direction of the trust. The trustee is not only there as a figurehead, but also for transferring or doing major things that the trust is involved in. The day-to-day activity of the trust could be conducted by the beneficial interest holders.

CHARITABLE REMAINDER TRUST

A rather remarkable and multi-faceted tool for sheltering assets and providing for a better retirement is often overlooked. It is a CRT or Charitable Remainder Trust.

Here's how it works. You take assets you wish to pass on to a charity upon your death and place them into the CRT. You retain the income from the trust and get a tax deduction now on the value of the gift. To determine the amount of the deduction, go to the IRS tables. The amount depends on the size of the gift and your actual life expectancy.

You can be the trustee of this trust and receive fees for this function. Let's assume you're in your 40s or 50s, and you don't particularly need any extra income at this time. You do, however, want to have more income when you are in your 60s. For the time being, have the trust invest in high growth but low income investments. Don't get me wrong, if you can find high growth/high income investments, do it. The size of the asset base grows, and then when it's time to retire, start switching the types of investments to high yield (income).

Why? Because now you can draw out income to retire. Let me show you how this part works. When you set up the trust, the language in the documents has you draw a percentage from the trust on at least an annual basis (usually on a quarterly basis). These fees paid to you are based on the value of the investments held in trust on the first day of the year. If there is not enough income, you should have a "make-up" clause allowing you to draw out the funds on a delayed basis.

Do you see why at first (the early years) the trust should invest in low yielding but highly appreciating investment vehicles? Now you ask, "How do I take current assets such as real estate and get them into cash to invest in these more liquid investments?" It's not difficult. I'll explain how and show you some tax angles, and then I'll pose a question you must think about.

Once the trust is set up (a matter of days) you simply deed or assign the property into the trust. For example, you purchased a fourplex many years ago for $100,000. Currently it is worth $440,000. This highly appreciated property is transferred and you get a whopping deduction of $440,000. Why so large? Remember you purchased this property many years ago; your mortgage is now paid off. Again, the size of the deduction is determined by the table and your life expectancy. Compare this to selling the property and then paying 28% (or about $100,000) to the IRS and then giving the balance to charity.

Once placed into trust, this property and other gifts could be sold. There are no tax consequences and the proceeds could be placed into more liquid and manageable investments. Remember, you are the trustee so you are in charge of the trust activities.

This type of trust acts as a tax-free retirement plan in this way. This trust is tax exempt, which means all the growth is tax free to the trust. However, when income is made it must be paid to the income beneficiary. Your ability to make these types of investment decisions puts you in control.

These are some drawbacks:

1) This trust is irrevocable. Pulling out excess income, or reverting assets to your personal name can disqualify the trust. Solution: don't place any assets into the trust which you think you'll need later.

2) The proceeds upon your death must go to a charity. You're entitled to the income while alive, but your children or grandchildren cannot get the trust assets later.

If you have desires to leave assets to children or grandchildren, provisions should be made through other trust arrangements, including a Living Trust or a Generation Skipping Trust. If, when you feel that those needs will be met and you still have desires to leave some to a charity, then this CRT may be just right. Also, if you need the tax deductions now, this could work nicely.

Back to our example. If you gift your highly appreciated property to the trust and create this large deduction, it could offset a larger capital gain on another property or other income. Let's say you have purchased another property for $200,000 and it sells for $500,000. You have a capital gain of $300,000 which will produce a tax liability of about $90,000. But you have a $300,000 deduction from the gift. Think about this. You gift a property to a deserving charity later. You get the deduction of up to 50% of your income now. This deduction offsets this income as you get the income for acting as trustee, the deduction could offset part of that income also.

Hopefully this investment and all your new investments will continue to grow. Current yields can be reinvested or paid out in fees. The purpose is to have as large of an investment as possible to finally turn over to the charity.

This structuring might look unfair to your heirs, but that may not necessarily be the case. Life insurance, if purchased properly in a well-structured trust, brings up a whole new dimension. The amount of the policy could equal everything your heirs would get anyway. Life insurance proceeds (if not part of your estate ownership) are not subject to estate taxes. If your estate is large, this CRT added benefit means you can pass along substantially more than the $600,000 exemption. Also, life insurance proceeds avoid all the administrative expense and hassles which normally beset assets passed through a typical estate settlement process.

> **SOME LIFE INSURANCE PROCEEDS ARE NOT SUBJECT TO ESTATE TAXES**

Also remember at some future time you can switch the investments so you can draw out your fees (to be spent in conjunction with other retirement income) and also the extra "make-up" fees not received in prior years.

If you use this type of trust for a retirement plan, remember there are no limitations to the number or value of the donations. There is a $2,000 maximum on an IRA and $30,000 in other pension plans. Another point: in the previous example, because the highly appreciated asset was later sold by the trust with no capital gains due, the entire $300,000 goes into investments.

What makes the CRT a different vehicle than other trusts is the very nature of the trust created by Congress and placed into the tax code. It is a "split interest" trust, simply meaning the income is split to the income beneficiary, and the principal (or donation and increased value thereon) is split to the charity beneficiary.

CRT IS A 'SPLIT INTEREST' TRUST

There are four types of Charitable Remainder Trusts.

1) **The Charitable Remainder Lead Trust**

   This trust is set up so the charity receives the income from the trust assets during the lifetime of the trust, but the assets placed into the trust revert back to the donor. The Charitable Lead Trust is subject to the generation skipping tax. I do not recommend it.

2) **The Charitable Remainder Annuity Trust (CRAT)**

   This trust allows for one donation into the trust. Payouts are established and the asset passes to the charity upon the death of the donor. Because you can only make one donation, I do not recommend this one.

3) **The Charitable Remainder Unitrust (CRUT)**

   CRUT IS BEST

   This trust allows for not only an initial donation, but subsequent donations. This is by far the most popular trust arrangement. I recommend this one.

4) Pooled Income Fund

This type of arrangement allows you to put your donations into a trust controlled by someone else. Your assets are pooled with other's assets. You receive your personal share of income. (We will not explore this one any further, as you are not in control.)

Let's return to number three. The CRUT requires that the income beneficiary receives at least 5% annually of the value of the assets (principal) held in trust. This amount could be 5 or 8%. The IRS has, in a private letter ruling, approved up to 15%. You have to make the choice of the percentage up front and once you do, it cannot be changed. The income pay out could be stipulated either for: 1) a specified number of years, or 2) for the life of one or more of the beneficiaries (owner, donor and/or spouse).

The date of the valuation of the assets should be January 1st or some date near the beginning of the year. If they are assets held in trust, stocks, or bonds, the valuation is simple, but if the assets are real estate or private business interest, something like an appraisal will have to be done. There are even variations of the Unitrust: 1) the standard Unitrust, 2) the "net" income Unitrust, and 3) the "net" income Unitrust, but with a make-up provision.

THE MAKE-UP PROVISION

If the lead trust or annuity trust does not have enough cash flow to pay out the 5%, the trustee would have to distribute assets or sell off some assets to get cash. However, with the Unitrust make-up provision, there need be no invasion of the principal. The payment is held in abeyance and paid out later.

What gives power to this trust as a potential "pension-type" instrument is you can control the type of investments. Isn't this what you wanted for the charity? Think about it. You convert the assets to high growth instruments. The body of the trust grows. No income is paid out (remember our example: you're younger—30 to 60—and don't need the income), but later where your income is lessened you convert the type of investments to pay out your 5 or 10% or even more to make up for the percentage you did not receive in prior years.

TRUSTEE

There is no stipulation in the tax code as to who can serve as trustee. You, as the donor, may function in this capacity. There is a letter ruling (7730015) where the donor was also the income beneficiary and served as trustee.

Furthermore, the IRS said (Revenue Ruling 80-83, 1980-1, C.B. 210) the donor could serve as a co-trustee when the funding is stock in a privately held corporation where he was a director of the corporation.

Remember, as trustee, you are in control of the assets: controlling the type of investments, the buying and selling, and all other important aspects of the trust. The purpose in setting up these trust arrangements is to:

YOU CONTROL THE TYPE OF INVESTMENTS

1) Empower you with the ability to make small or large contributions to the charity of your choice.

2) Provide controllable income now and possibly even more later on (see make-up provision).

3) Seriously reduce or possibly eliminate estate taxes on these particular deductible donations.

4) Save money on taxes immediately by employing the tax deductibility of these donations.

If you have assets and they are growing in value every year, this creates a little larger estate tax planning problem. Now, however, all these gifted assets are growing without the worry of the tax consequences later.

You can change the trust's beneficiary any time you like, and it can have several beneficiaries (or you could set up separate trusts). The CRT can be combined with the $600,000 one-time exclusion, the $10,000 per year gifting rules, and the Living Trust. Owner-ship minimizing through corporations and Lim-ited Partnerships means your heirs or chosen char-ity will get everything.

OTHER TRUSTS–A BRIEF OVERVIEW

1) Credit Shelter Trust

This is sometimes called a Bypass Trust. This is a trust set up to bypass the spouse's estate and make sure your whole $600,000 passes on to your heirs. The spouse can also pass on $600,000. If you give everything to the spouse, they are still limited to $600,000. This is ex-actly what an A–B Trust will do in a typical Living Trust.

2) Spendthrift Trust

If you are worried about a certain child wast-ing money, or if you are worried that poten-tial creditors could attack your assets (or those directly owned by your children), or if you are worried about one of your children get-ting a divorce, then you could set up this trust. It's a simple trust that holds assets. Later the trust can distribute assets or income (even in installments) to whomever you wish.

If a trust makes money, taxes are due. If it sells something, taxes are due. They are good for secrecy and for lawsuit protection, but they can-not be used in and of themselves as a tax avoid-ance or tax reduction vehicle.

Chapter Twelve

Putting It All Together

"A taxpaying public that does not understand the law is a taxpaying public that cannot comply with the law."

–former IRS Commissioner Lawrence B. Gibbs

Entity structuring is quite simple, yet the ramifications of wise entity structuring will be quite dynamic and far reaching: you cannot only have a diversity of investments and business interests; you must also have a diversity of entities owning or controlling those same investments. Lets recap each entity here:

> **This is the POWERHOUSE**

Corporation

This is the backbone of your family enterprise, and the workhorse that adds so much to everything else.

1) It is perpetual—it does not die.
2) Different classes of stock can be issued.
3) Different voting rights can be applied to the different shares.
4) The officers are protected.
5) Shareholders have no personal liability.
6) It has incredible tax advantages:
   a) Works with a pension plan.

b) Can have fiscal year-end different from December 31st.

c) Can make forgivable loan.

d) Can make deductible investments.

e) Operates multiple businesses.

f) Can be established in Nevada to take advantage of laws there.

g) Can deduct travel for business—for attending meetings, et cetera.

h) Can be "S" or "C" corporation and receive tax benefits.

7) It protects assets.

8) It is an estate planning tool.

9) Can own stock in other corporations or units in Limited Partnerships.

LIVING TRUST

The Umbrella Entity.

1) Helps avoid probate—saves time, money, exposure.

2) Provides some estate planning

3) Saves on estate taxes.

4) Allows for stepped-up basis to avoid capital gains taxes.

5) Provides for smooth transition of business enterprise.

6) Allows you to provide for children and grandchildren or charities.

LIVING TRUST
AS `UMBRELLA´

PENSION PLAN

Work hard, retire rich.

1) Provides a tax haven.

2) Like a forced savings plan.

3) Donations are tax deductible.

4) Investments grow tax free until distributed.

5) Safety is unsurpassed.

6) Borrowing money allowed for certain items.

7) Combination of plans allows for maximum contribution—up to $30,000 in defined contribution.

8) "Self-trusteed"—you control everything.

LIMITED PARTNERSHIP

A different entity for different purposes.

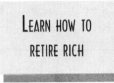

LEARN HOW TO
RETIRE RICH

1) Good for families with large asset base.

2) Can use several at one time to control different investments.

3) Works nicely with the corporate structure.

4) Allows maximum and effective use of the gift giving rules.

5) Difficult for creditors to get at assets.

6) Offers superior methods for distributing income to children for tax savings (unearned income).

DIVERSITY
OF USES

7) Can own stock in corporations or units in other partnerships.

8) Can be used in conjunction with corporation for maximum tax benefits, i.e. Corporation as General Partner.

9) Distribution is considered "unearned income" and is not subject to Social Security taxes.

CHARITABLE REMAINDER TRUST
Deductions and many benefits later.

1) Used for tax planning now. Donations of certain investments to charity.

2) Special rule allows for "pension-type" aspect—draws out substantial income later.

3) Protects family's interests.

4) Lessens your "taxable estate" and saves money.

Most of you need three or four of these different entities. They work together, not alone. From the different audio seminars in my Financial Fortress System, you'll learn how to integrate and use the various entities.

Because of the nature or function of each particular entity, they work with each other. I'll give one "typical" example here. Note the letters. You'll be able to follow along as you read the points after the diagram.

AN INTEGRATION OF ENTITIES
This is the Lincoln family (see following diagram). Dave has a manufacturing company. It's worth about $700,000 and produces about $180,000 of net profits this year. It's growing quite rapidly and takes a lot of his time. This company owns about $110,000 of equipment. This is a high risk business and he is constantly worried about lawsuits. They have three children. Marcie, his wife, has a typesetting business. She works part-time and has one other part-time employee. It has $40,000 worth of equipment. She nets about $25,000 a year. Her business is a sole proprietorship.

USE 'PENSION' ASPECT FOR DYNAMIC RESULTS

Their home is worth $280,000, with an $80,000 mortgage. They have no formal retirement plan, but do have $8,500 in IRAs. They own a cabin in the mountains worth $40,000.

They have stock investments of $45,000 in their personal name. They have a duplex (free and clear) worth $40,000 and two other rental houses with combined equities of $80,000.

Dave's brother has a software company worth $300,000. Dave's share is 35% or $105,000, because he put up $40,000 to help fund the business. He draws no money now but expects some in a few years.

This year they'll pay about $45,000 in taxes.

You can see they:

1) Have no serious lawsuit protection strategies (only liability insurance).

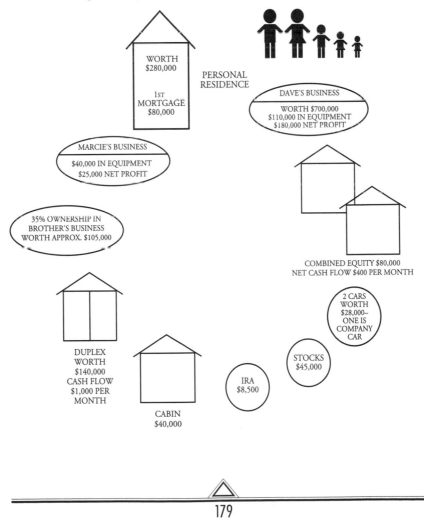

a) One lawsuit could ruin everything.

b) Possible liability for brother's debts.

2) Have no serious tax planning vehicles.
   a) Some into IRA.

   b) Sole Proprietorship.

      (1) No diversion of funds—year end, et cetera.

      (2) No corporate brackets.

      (3) All income to one bracket.

      (4) Could use Charitable Remainder Trust.

3) Have no estate planning vehicles.
   a) No Stock Splitting.

   b) No Living Trust.

   c) No Charitable Remainder Trust.

4) Have no serious pension planning.
   a) No KEOGH or, better yet, corporate pension plan.

   b) No tax deductions.

   c) No tax free growth.

   d) No control.

You may be seeing something like this for the first time. Don't let it confuse you. You'll soon see the logic behind each move. Don't expect your CPA or financial planner to understand this. They're locked into their old, ineffective wrap. It will take you one-half to one full hour to grasp all the implications and ramifications of integrating entities. It will take them weeks because they have to undo so much wrong information that they've fed into their brains for 20 years.

Remember, we're not here for quick fixes or band-aids. We are taking a "holistic" approach to complete wealth enhancement, entity integration, tax strategies, retirement planning and estate structuring. Also, you'll be an integral part in setting this up.

I once met a couple with 12 children. I asked them how they kept track of all their names. They looked at me like I was crazy. They rattled them off so fast I barely caught one. Likewise this will be your family of entities. You know them by what they do—their functions. You'll have nicknames for each entity like TOP for Technical Optional Products, Inc. You'll love seeing your growth, keeping tax money working for you, and retirement accounts building—all protected and ready to meet any contingency.

The following list and diagrams on the next few pages show Dave and Marcie Lincoln's entity integration.

A) Your personal residence should be assigned to your Living Trust.
1) Unless you're really susceptible to lawsuits (then perhaps a Family Limited Partnership.)
2) Residence goes to stepped up basis if one spouse dies and the other spouse sells property. But that's not all; all property— stock, units, rentals, or other investments go to the stepped up basis if owned in a Living Trust.
3) Equity should be encumbered—see "N."

B) Cabin—put in Living Trust.

C) Stocks—put in Living Trust.
1) Assign either individual stocks or whole brokerage account to Living Trust
2) Possibly divvy up to other corporations.
   a) Trade stock—public for private.

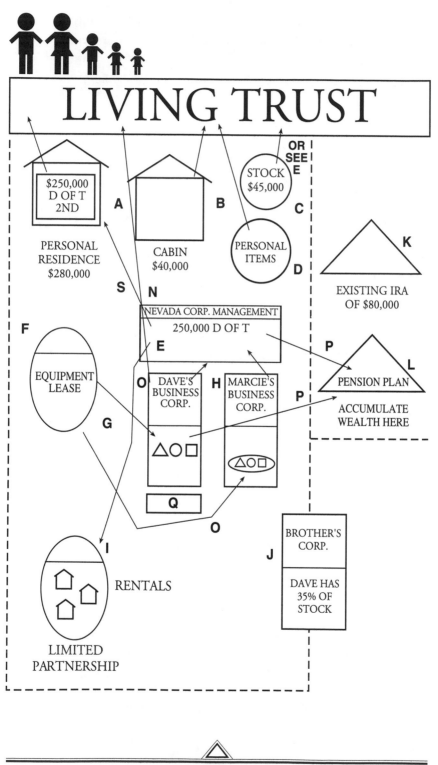

LIVING TRUST

$250,000
D OF T
2ND

A

B

STOCK
$45,000

OR
SEE
E

C

PERSONAL
RESIDENCE
$280,000

CABIN
$40,000

PERSONAL
ITEMS

D

K

EXISTING IRA
OF $80,000

S

N

NEVADA CORP. MANAGEMENT
250,000 D OF T

E

P

F

EQUIPMENT
LEASE

O

DAVE'S
BUSINESS
CORP.

H

MARCIE'S
BUSINESS
CORP.

P

L

PENSION PLAN

ACCUMULATE
WEALTH HERE

G

△○□

△○□

Q

O

I

RENTALS

J

BROTHER'S
CORP.

DAVE HAS
35% OF
STOCK

LIMITED
PARTNERSHIP

    b) If dividends are taken—take advantage of 70% Exclusion Rule.

D) Personal Items—assign to Schedule A of Living Trust.

E) Management Corporation—Nevada.
1) Move money—deduct—to "no tax" state.
2) Could own property, but should not own too much. This entity is a "cash flow" entity.
3) Manage other corporations—by contract.
4) General partner for Limited Partnership.
5) Put lien on personal residence to encumber equity.
6) If you do "5," try to make name like a bank, i.e. "Capital Funding Corporation."
7) Put money into corporate Pension Plan.

F) Limited Partnership—equipment leasing.
1) Buy, hold, lease equipment to corporation.
2) Corporations lease or rent.

G) Big Corporation.
1) Divvy up stock to children or others.
2) Pay management company—Nevada.
3) Pay leasing company for equipment.
4) Don't own equipment.
5) Consider even putting land (building) in separate Limited Partnership.
6) Try to establish as many independent contractors as possible instead of employees.
7) Pay money to pension fund or see "E."

H) Corporation (Nevada)—Typesetting.

1) Avoid personal liability.

2) Tax structure—fiscal year end and lower brackets.

3) Lease equipment from Limited Partnership—Equipment Leasing.

4) Pay money to management corporation (or keep, if lower bracket).

5) Possibly have own pension fund.

I) Limited Partnership.

1) Own existing rentals.

2) Let corporation be general partner—avoid personal liability.

3) Initially issue all assets to Dave and Marcie (Living Trust Schedule A).

4) Gift units ($10,000 worth per year) to each child or hold in trust for them.

J) Brother's Business.

1) Should be corporation for all the above reasons. Dave and Marcie avoid liability.

2) Dave's percentage of ownership assigned to other entities—Living Trust is a good bet. Could be other corporations or directly to children.

K) IRA.

1) Keep separate.

2) Review beneficiary pay out (see if different combinations work).

3) Keep adding more.

L) Pension Account.
1) Set up and contribute as much as possible.

2) Include employer—consider 401(k) of corporation G.

3) Take aggressive stance with money in plan later as current business demands so much.

4) Get investment with high growth—diversify later.

M) Management corporation to be general partner of Family Limited Partnership.

N) Lien.
1) Dave and Marcie have too much equity—a big target.

2) Trade stock for a mortgage. Record it so there is no equity available.

3) Every homeowner should "homestead" their house to protect equity.

O) Limited Partnership leases equipment to corporation.
1) It earns money.

2) Pay money to children to avoid dividend (double taxation) treatment.

P) Pay (contribute) money to pension funds.
1) Fully deductible—great tax savings.

Q) Own land, but keep building as separate entity—corporation leases building from partnership.

1) If the corporation folded, the building is still controlled—the equipment is owned by Limited Partnership—Equipment Leasing. The corporation has cash flow, but no substantial assets.

Because of the net profits and value of the entities (business assets), Dave and Marcie are strong candidates for a Charitable Remainder Trust.

Now review the next diagram. Note what we don't put inside trust:

A) Pension Plan.

B) CRT—Charitable Remainder Trust.

Also, just because we have a corporation drawn inside the trust does not mean it controls the corporation. In reality, Dave and Marcie's stock holdings are the items owned by the trust.

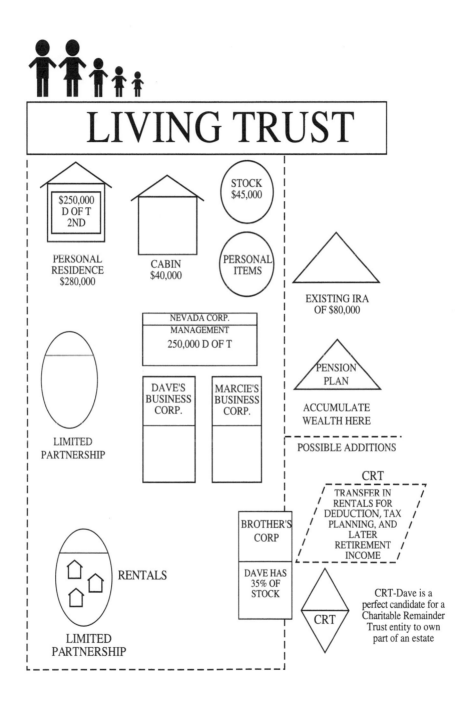

Conclusion

I wish I had had this information fifteen years ago. It is mind boggling to think of the problems I could have solved and the taxes I could have saved.

I wrote this book as something I would like to own and read myself. Its primary purpose is to educate you, but secondarily to help you educate your tax advising professionals. That's a tough assignment, as many of them are locked in their old ways of, "Well, you'll have to pay taxes on that."

You probably can't imagine how much research and "on the street" experience it takes to learn and formulate these techniques. I've been blessed with meeting some of the greatest entrepreneurs, educators, and leaders in America. Each one has added another layer of knowledge or wisdom.

Wisdom is the proper application of knowledge. My goal was to give you wisdom that will bring effective results. That's why I not only tell the why of incorporating but the how. That's why I not only teach information about each entity or strategy, but the "how to's" of integrating and using them synergistically.

There is not one set road map for each of us. Life is a journey—a wonderful, trial and error, success and failure, "pick yourself up and get on with it" adventure. In the business world, this is especially true. New opportunities keep arising. Old ideas fade away or are revived. The target is usually moving. Health problems and age change many previously cherished goals. Having children literally changes the nature of our concerns and what we view as important. Many times we are affected by events outside our direct control, and experience profound consequences.

But such is the nature and challenge of living. And while there is no set road map, there are definitely "good, better, and best" ways of traveling.

1) You can travel on well-established roads or take the long, hard way.

2) You can stop and sight-see once in a while if you leave yourself plenty of time.

3) There are "guides" available—people who have been there before. The most accomplished professionals and successful people have mentors—coaches, if you will—to help them see things they may not have seen themselves.

4) You can definitely choose the type of vehicle you'll use, and whether you'll make the trip with one car or a caravan.

5) You can prepare, in advance, for most contingencies.

6) You can determine alternate routes if your first choice doesn't work.

7) You can usually choose your traveling companions.

8) And definitely you can enjoy more of the fruits of your labors and then pass on to family members or others more of what you worked so hard to accumulate.

Usually the most powerful ideas are the simplest and easiest to implement. The very nature of the wealth accumulation process requires a certain amount of chaos, uncertainty, and dedication to fundamental principles such as leverage, monitoring activity, active participation of many people, and methods for targeting results. You don't need an extra layer of burdens. That is precisely why different legal structures are needed: to make sure, in a low maintenance way, you have the freedom to "go for it," knowing that the foundation is secure and the framework is strong.

Each entity has a place. You'll use one as a cash flow entity, another for holding assets for your posterity, one for retirement, and another to make sure everything passes on without a hitch. Your need for one entity may come and go. You may want to use one to encumber "equity" in another. One may help you save in-state taxes, while another lets you invest and do business worldwide.

Ultimately, what most of us are trying to achieve is some mystical, financial freedom—mystical only in that many have confused it with happiness. You've heard the expression, "Money doesn't buy happiness." Well, neither does poverty. I'd rather have the problems associated with wealth, than with poverty. And what does this have to do with money and taxes and legal structures? A lot. Wealth means a certain degree of safety.

As I look over my adult life and think of the many endeavors I've engaged in—safety and security have been really important. The irony is this: whenever I invested in something or started a business to provide financial security, it usually backfired. Conversely, when I've tried something which required risk and no certain return, I excelled. You're never going to get rich on a particular investment if you know your rate of return. Think this through. If a CD is paying 5.27%, it is not an investment which will make you wealthy. When you buy a property, or invest in a stock or start a business, you don't know how much you'll make; hence there is great potential for wealth.

If the last statement is true, and in most cases I think it is, then you can obtain more if you effectively use the law of leverage—for instance a $10,000 down payment on a $100,000 rental home. The other side of the leverage coin is debt. The avoidance of things uncertain, risk, and debt cause most people to stagnate financially.

You're not reading this book or listening to the taped seminars because you're lazy or afraid of sticking out. You want the better things in life and the time to enjoy them. You know one good piece of information applied consistently brings success. You know knowledge is power.

Your retirement is too close; your family is too important; your business income and structuring are too important to leave anything up to chance. You need to get financially fit for the opportunity and then within the framework of a sound financial structure, do all the things you want to do!

In closing, I would like to share my thoughts on what wealth really is. I used to think it was a few million dollars, or excess cash flow. The years have taught me many lessons. As I look at my own life and the lives of countless others and try to ascertain what happiness is, it strikes me again and again that wealth is service to others. There is no reward in being selfish. The reward is in relationships. To me, helping the lives of others is true wealth. If I can help you run your business properly, structure your affairs to maximize potential, and aid you in the ability to give more—then my mission as an educator is fulfilled.

Appendix One

Case Studies

Case Study #1

Meet Dave, a young go-getter who really took to real estate after coming to one of my seminars. He bought and sold a few properties following the Money Machine method. He also got involved with several apartment buildings with a friend and two investors.

He and his friend made deals to operate the buildings for a split of the ownership and some of the cash flow. The arrangement was a loose one for this management company. Nothing was in writing. They owned a certain percentage of buildings, sometimes together, sometimes separately. Each paid out different amounts because some didn't even have a positive cash flow. Also, no clear plan was set for the disposition of the properties or business.

Anyone in business consulting has heard this story many times, and usually it ends up in failure. I was impressed with Dave's energy and drive. He knew he had a small problem that could mushroom.

He also had a few small investments and other miscellaneous things with no significant value.

I have several problems with these arrangements. Unless properly drawn up and expertly run, partnerships are sinking ships, and this type of partnership is the worst. A loose confederation, a joint venture with no legal structure and all the ear-markings of disaster. For Dave this means potential problems. But why in the world would a person, Mr. Silent Part-

His assets look something like this:

NOTE $18,000	NOTE $13,300	NOTE $12,200
$192 NET PER MONTH	$145 NET PER MONTH	$100 NET PER MONTH, $150 PER MONTH AFTER 2 YEARS

JOB: COMPUTER SALESMAN EARNING $22,000 A YEAR
CASH: $8,000 FROM PROPERTY SALE PROCEEDS

16 UNIT BLDG.
17% OWNERSHIP
GEORGE, DAVE
23% FRIENDS SHARE
60% TO SILENT
PARTNER

VALUE $450,000
LOAN 320,000
EQUITY $130,000

NET CASH FLOW $900

*ALL NAMES ON TITLE

12 UNIT BLDG.

21% OWNERSHIP
25& GEORGE
55% TO Mr. S. P.

VALUE $400,000
LOAN 350,000
EQUITY $ 50,000

NO NET CASH FLOW

PROPERTY
MANAGEMENT CO.
(NEW–JUST
SETTING UP)

NO NET YET

22 UNIT BLDG.

21% OWNERSHIP
55% TO Mr. S. P.

VALUE $1,200,000
LOAN 900,000
EQUITY $300,000

NET CASH FLOW
$2,000

ner, put his money into investments in this format? General partnerships should be outlawed. The partners could by extension be responsible for each other's debts. Death of one ends the partnership, et cetera.

Mr. Silent Partner has much more at risk than the other two because it's his cash and if anything goes wrong, he has the deep pockets—a potential target. I'd like to cross-design all of them, but it would get too complicated. I'll just cross-design Dave and then give a few suggestions on what the other two could do.

Dave sees that more could be made if he owned it all, or at least found his own investor. He also believes that property management is the way to go. He is married with two small children. His design is on the following page.

LIVING TRUST OTHERS

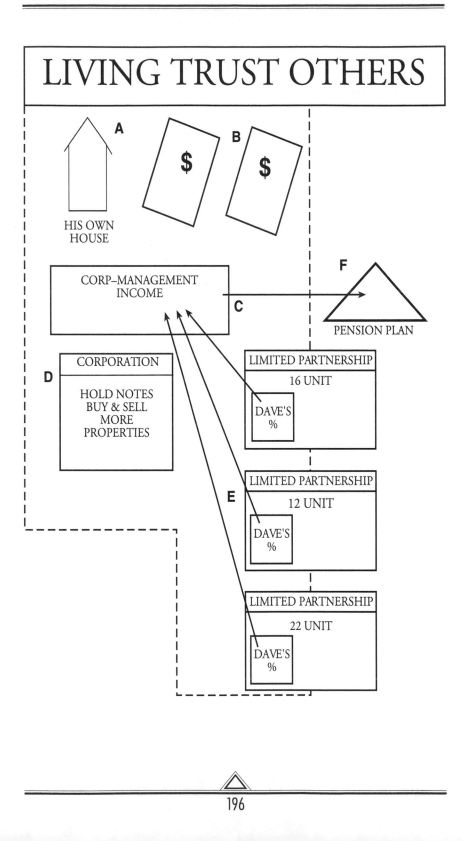

A HIS OWN HOUSE

B $ $

C CORP–MANAGEMENT INCOME

F PENSION PLAN

D CORPORATION

HOLD NOTES
BUY & SELL
MORE
PROPERTIES

LIMITED PARTNERSHIP

16 UNIT

DAVE'S %

E LIMITED PARTNERSHIP

12 UNIT

DAVE'S %

LIMITED PARTNERSHIP

22 UNIT

DAVE'S %

A) Own residence in Living Trust.

B) Other small assets in personal name or trust.

C) Set up Management Corporation. Hold no assets—pass through cash flow. Sponsor pension. Eventually, income source to replace job.

D) Hold existing notes and use to buy and sell more properties or notes. Once it hits $200,000 in net worth, set up new one.

E) Dave should have all properties owned in at least a Limited Partnership (or corporation), preferably three separate ones. If partners are not willing to restructure this, then Dave should set up a completely new and different corporation and assign his interest to it.

F) Pension Plan receives money from the Corporation and hopefully the proceeds from the plan where he currently works when he quits there.

Suggestions:

1) All three should restructure everything. Separate ownership from management.

2) All three should clearly write out their business plan: responsibility, liability, disposition, contingencies, et cetera.

3) All three should financially design themselves to avoid liability and the payment of extra taxes. If they like doing business together, why hinder that if one needs cash.

Example: Mr. Silent Partner has good losses now, but in three years he sells something else and needs to sell the 22 units. Dave and George don't want to. They should have buy-out rights or other ways of exiting this arrangement.

SUMMARY

Dave could grow faster with less liability exposure and taxes if he were properly structured. Also, his wife Karen wanted to get involved. She's now running the management company and handling the records and always looking for new properties.

CASE STUDY #2

This next account makes me a little angry. Read on and find out why. Emily had no legal structure at all. Here is her situation: she is married and has two older boys. The family owns 160 acres—four 40-acre tracks (sections) in the Tenecula/Rancho, California area. Each 40 acres was worth about $160,000 to $200,000. Their private residence was on one of the sections. The property was free and clear.

They also owned a fencing company doing about $400,000 a year—netting between $160,000 and $180,000. Her husband and son and two part-time employees worked the business.

Emily is 54 and worried because they have so little set aside for retirement. They have about $25,000 in other investments. Here's how they look:

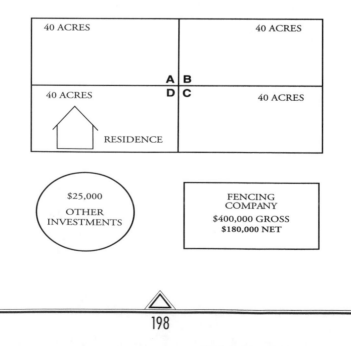

She learned about Living Trusts, protection and tax strategies afforded by a Nevada Corporation and most importantly about having a pension account.

She really needs four or five corporations—one for each section and definitely one for the fencing business (where there is a lot of exposure). She possibly doesn't need one for the 40 acres where their home is. That could be held in their Living Trust or indirectly in a Limited Partnership.

Also, she sees the company on a treadmill. She wants to free up some cash, do some real estate deals (which they had successfully done in the past), and particularly buy some high cash flow second mortgages. And then through that company or in combination with the fencing company, they can sock aside as much as possible into a Pension Plan.

They would look like this:

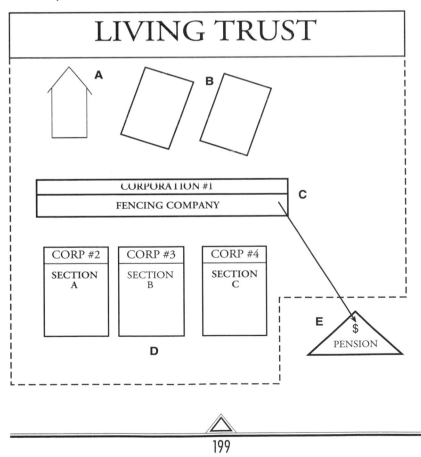

Explanation of the letters:

A) Have home or Section C in Living Trust or Family Limited Partnership.

B) Personal bank account and personal effects in Living Trust.

C) Fencing Company as a corporation.

D) Three corporations or limited partnerships for sections of land.

E) Pension account.

There is another way to do this that would allow paying an extra expense out of the corporation operating in California.

We didn't do anything with the equipment in the fencing company. Let's set up a leasing company (Limited Partnership) to own equipment and rent or lease purchase. Now no one can take it away, and we create another lower taxable entity. It would look like the following diagram.

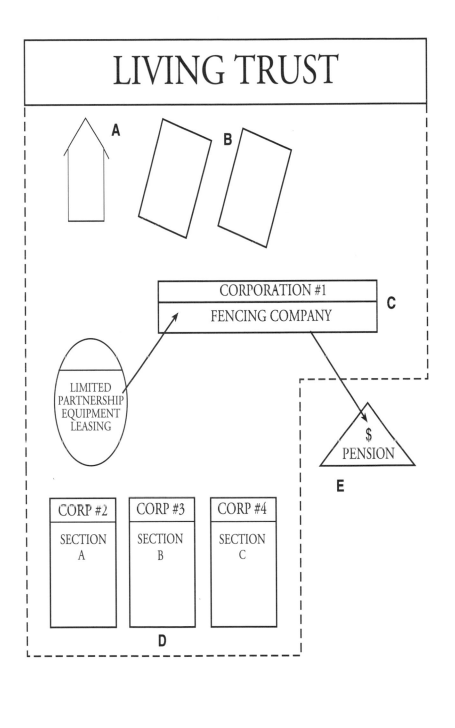

LIVING TRUST

A

B

CORPORATION #1

FENCING COMPANY

C

LIMITED
PARTNERSHIP
EQUIPMENT
LEASING

$
PENSION

E

CORP #2	CORP #3	CORP #4
SECTION A	SECTION B	SECTION C

D

Now the problem: Emily could only afford one corporation, one pension and one Living Trust, and those were to be paid for and set up over a three-month period of time.

She ran the idea past her CPA, which only served to unravel her plan. He mentioned that transferring a property (section B, as it didn't directly adjunct her 40-acre home section and it was the one she was to sell) into the corporation would trigger a property tax increase.

She sheepishly asked, "How much?" He answered, "Well, maybe $10,000." Now you understand this is all a maybe. "I've helped thousands of Californians set up corporations and transfer properties and not once, I repeat, not once has it done this." She continued, "But he has hundreds of successful clients and has been a CPA for 18 years." This only tells me he's been doing things the wrong way for 18 years.

He didn't even have the courage to call and discuss it. All his surmising just caused doubts. Time out! I refuse to recommend bandaids. We're talking about a lifetime financial plan here.

1) Ownership transferred and available for easy transfer in the future.

2) Stepped up basis to avoid tax in the Living Trust.

3) Living Trust to avoid probate.

4) Gifting ease with stocks and units.

5) Tax brackets lowered.

6) Money to lower tax jurisdiction.

7) Pension planning.

8) Liability Protection.

9) Asset enhancement.

10) A host of other benefits and uses available.

Two days before, Emily was happy and excited to finally get structured. She saw the benefits and advantages and she was ready, willing, and able to now control her financial destiny. But this one doubt remained. She canceled everything while she "thought it over." Now because of the one CPA, she has no Living Trust, no Pension Plan, no corporate tax or liability protection—nothing.

CASE STUDY #3

Michael was looking down the barrel of a major problem. He and two others started a computer software company five years ago. There is virtually a zero cost basis. A public company is now buying them out for $6,000,000. His share is 30% or $1,800,000. Capital Gains will be around $500,000. And that's not all. He started another private firm on the side, and he and his wife take home about $140,000 a year. It is also a corporation.

Michael came through my Wealth Academy in November. The sale was to take place in December. They also owned twenty acres and three rentals with an equity value of $110,000 total. Personal effects and things totaled $75,000.

Well, there's no way at this late date to hide all that capital gain. The main company has a Pension Plan. Upon termination, he can take the $80,000 (his portion) and put it into a Pension Plan. If we had met years before, all this stock would have been placed into several entities with his children indirectly owning it. Look at his design on the following page:

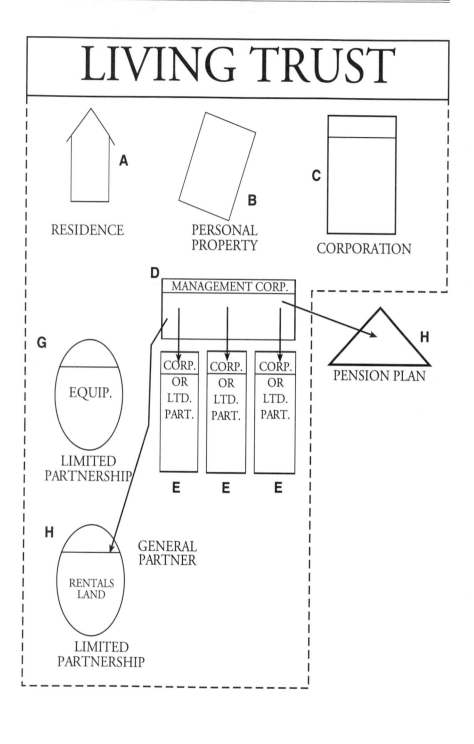

LIVING TRUST

A RESIDENCE

B PERSONAL PROPERTY

C CORPORATION

D MANAGEMENT CORP.

G EQUIP. LIMITED PARTNERSHIP

E CORP. OR LTD. PART.

E CORP. OR LTD. PART.

E CORP. OR LTD. PART.

H PENSION PLAN

H GENERAL PARTNER

RENTALS LAND LIMITED PARTNERSHIP

[Note: do you notice that we don't put a trust in a trust?]

Explanation of the letters:

A) Home: deed to Living Trust. He had not done this yet.

B) Personal effects: deed to Living Trust.

C) This is the entity he and his wife are working. After the sale, this will become even bigger and be the focus of most of their activity.

D) Management Corporation to consult with or manage different entities.

E) Three Corporations, maybe five or six. Immediately do a stock swap with existing company (the one being bought.) This should have happened five years ago so it wouldn't raise red flags. Maybe it's too late. Have ownership, director totally different—maybe even use different legal structures like the Family Partnership. Corporation is best, in this case only for ease of exchange stock.

F) Family Limited Partnership for owning rentals and holding land.

G) Limited Partnership for leasing equipment to Corporation C.

H) Pension account for receipt of funds from qualified plan and new donation from D.

Michael is now having his parents own certain corporations. The sale was extended one year, and entity and tax restraints saved Michael and Joan about $24,000.

Appendix Two

Legend

I use these symbols in laying out custom designs for individuals and companies, or individuals with many companies or investments. Hopefully you will see a format here that works for you. I realize how difficult it is to set yourself up on a piece of paper. The exercise is beneficial though–you get to see the flow of money, ownership and control.

You can make copies of the following pages to diagram your own situation.

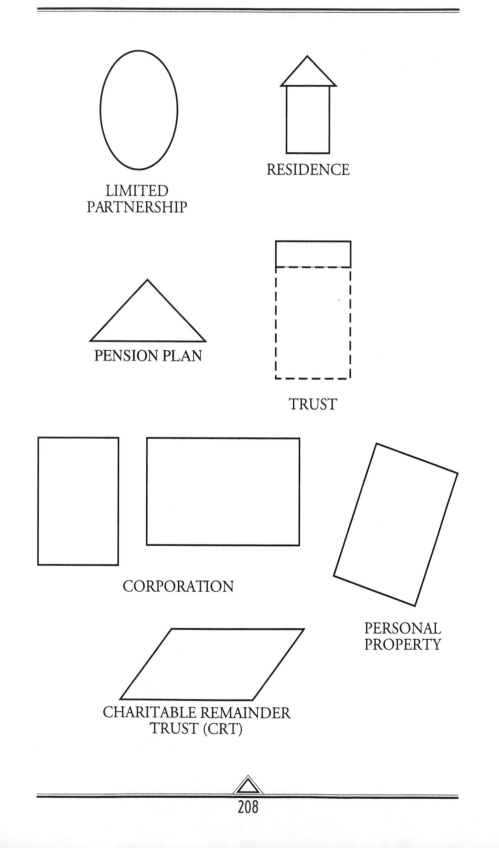

LIMITED
PARTNERSHIP

RESIDENCE

PENSION PLAN

TRUST

CORPORATION

PERSONAL
PROPERTY

CHARITABLE REMAINDER
TRUST (CRT)

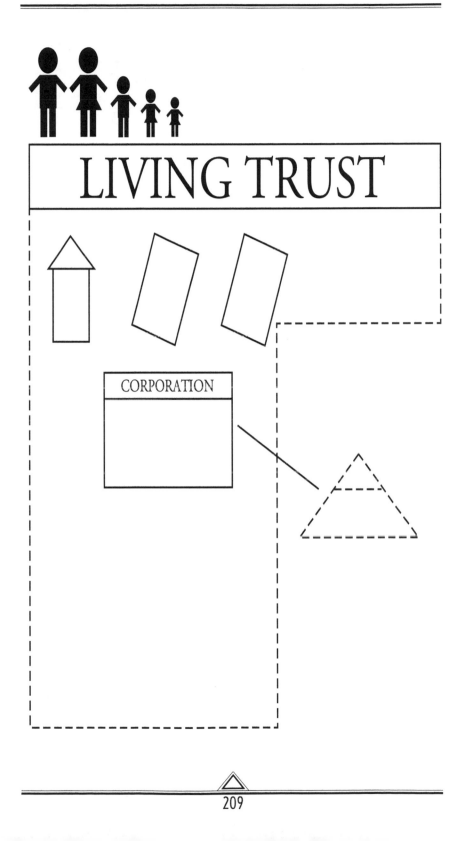

LIVING TRUST

CORPORATION

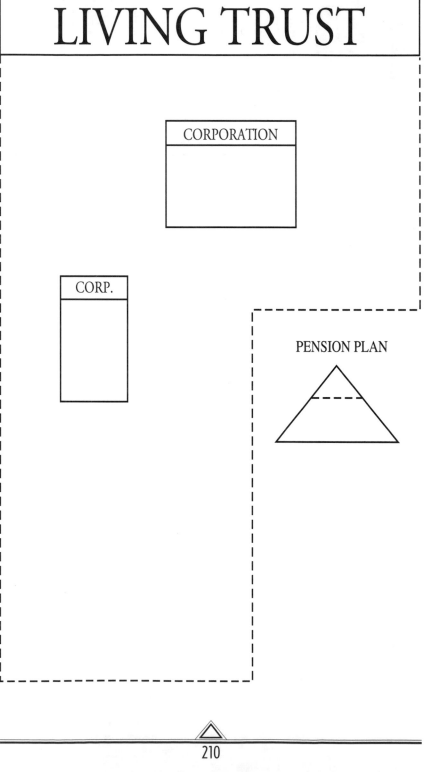

LIVING TRUST

CORPORATION

CORP.

PENSION PLAN

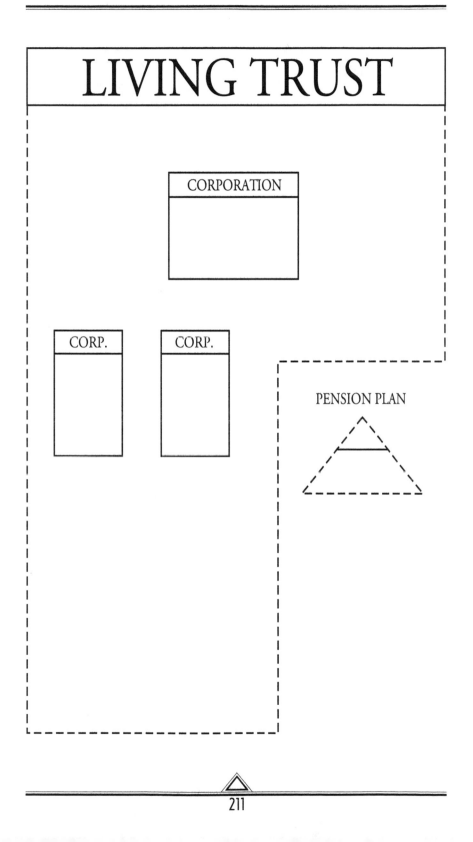

LIVING TRUST

CORPORATION

CORP.

CORP.

PENSION PLAN

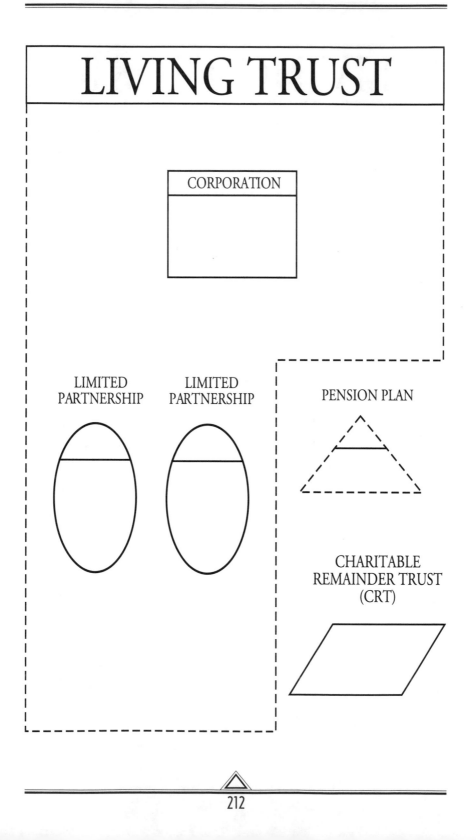

LIVING TRUST

CORPORATION

LIMITED PARTNERSHIP

LIMITED PARTNERSHIP

PENSION PLAN

CHARITABLE REMAINDER TRUST (CRT)

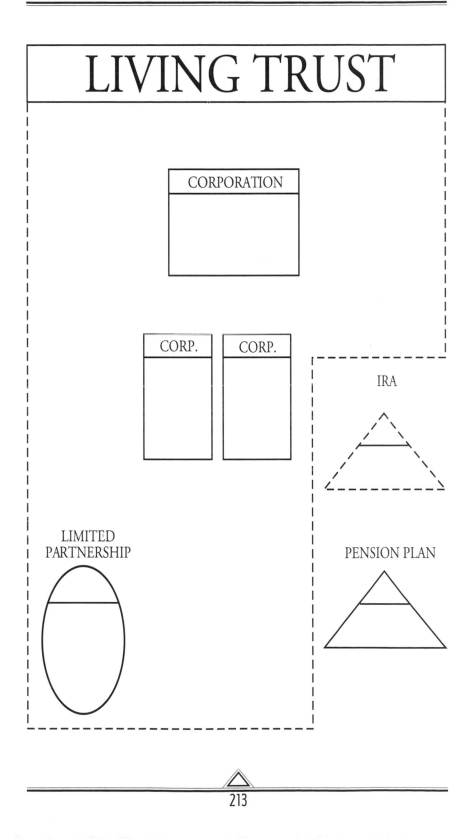

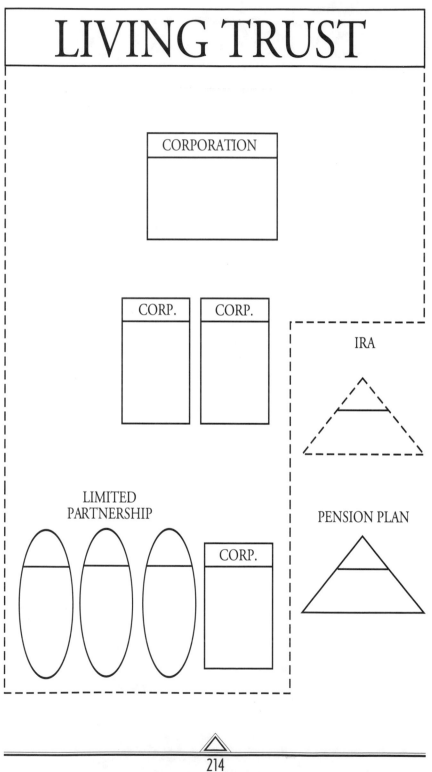

LIVING TRUST

CORPORATION

CORP.

CORP.

IRA

LIMITED PARTNERSHIP

CORP.

PENSION PLAN

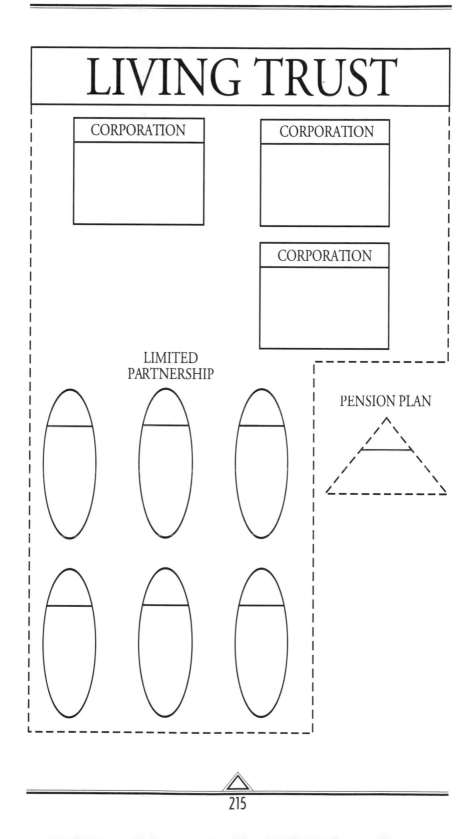

Appendix Three

Available Resources

The following books, videos, and audiocassettes have been reviewed by the Wade Cook Seminars staff and are suggested as reading and resource material for continuing education to help with your real estate and stock market investments. Because new ideas and techniques come along and laws change, we're always updating our catalog.

To order a copy of our current catalog, please write or call us at:

Wade Cook Seminars, Inc.
14675 Interurban Avenue South
Seattle, Washington 98168-4664
1–800–872–7411

Or, visit us on our web sites at:

www.wadecook.com

www.lighthousebooks.com

Also, we would love to hear your comments on our products and services, as well as your testimonials on how these products have benefited you. We look forward to hearing from you!

STOCK MARKET

INCOME FORMULAS—A FREE CASSETTE
By Wade B. Cook

Learn the 11 cash flow formulas taught in the Wall Street Workshop. Learn to double your money every $2^1/2$ to 4 months.

WALL STREET MONEY MACHINE
By Wade B. Cook

Appearing on the *New York Times* Business Best Sellers list for over one year, **Wall Street Money Machine** contains the best strategies for wealth enhancement and cash flow creation you'll find anywhere. Throughout this book, Wade Cook describes many of his favorite strategies for generating cash flow through the stock market: Rolling Stock, Proxy Investing, Covered Calls, and many more. It's a great introduction for creating wealth using the Wade Cook formulas.

STOCK MARKET MIRACLES
By Wade B. Cook

The anxiously-awaited partner to **Wall Street Money Machine**, this book has proven to be just as invaluable. **Stock Market Miracles** improves on some of the strategies from **Wall Street Money Machine**, as well as introducing new and valuable twists on our old favorites.

BEAR MARKET BALONEY
By Wade B. Cook

A more timely book wouldn't be possible. Wade's predictions came true while the book was at press! Don't miss this insightful look into what makes bull and bear markets and how to make exponential returns in any market.

DYNAMIC DOLLARS VIDEO
By Wade B. Cook

Wade Cook's 90 minute introduction to the basics of his Wall Street formulas and strategies. In this presentation designed especially for video, Wade explains the meter drop philosophy, Rolling Stock, basics of Proxy Investing, and Writing Covered Calls. Perfect for anyone looking for a little basic information.

ZERO TO ZILLIONS
By Wade B. Cook

This is a powerful audio workshop on Wall Street—understanding the stock market game, playing it successfully, and retiring rich. Learn eleven powerful investment strategies to avoid pitfalls and losses, catch "Day Trippers," "Bottom Fish," write Covered Calls, double your money in one week on options on stock split companies, and so much more. Wade "Meter Drop" Cook will teach you how he makes fantastic annual returns in this, so that you can do likewise.

THE WALL STREET WORKSHOP VIDEO SERIES
By Wade B. Cook

If you can't make it to the Wall Street Workshop soon, get a head start with these videos. Ten albums containing eleven hours of intense instruction on Rolling Stock, Options on stock split companies, writing Covered Calls, and eight other tested and proven strategies designed to help you earn *18% per month* on your investments. By learning, reviewing, and implementing the strategies taught here, you will gain the knowledge and the confidence to take control of your investments, and double their value every $2^1/_2$ to 4 months.

THE NEXT STEP VIDEO SERIES
By Team Wall Street

The advanced version of the Wall Street Workshop. Full of power-packed strategies from Wade Cook, this is not a duplicate of the Wall Street Workshop, but a very important partner. The methods taught in this seminar will supercharge the strategies taught in the Wall Street Workshop and teach you even more ways to make more money! In the *Next Step*, you'll learn how to find the stocks to fit the formulas through technical analysis, fundamentals, home trading tools, and more.

WEALTH INFORMATION NETWORK (WIN)

This subscription internet service provides you with the latest financial formulas and updated entity structuring strategies. New, timely information is entered several times a day. Wade Cook and his Team Wall Street staff write for WIN, giving you updates on their own current stock plays, companies who announced earnings, companies who announced stock splits, and the latest trends in the market.

WIN is also divided into categories according to specific strategies and contains archives of all our trades so you can view our history. If you are just getting started in the stock market, this is a great way to follow people who are doubling their money every $2^1/2$ to 4 months. If you are experienced already, it's the way to confirm your feelings and research with others who are generating wealth through the stock market.

Subscribing to *WIN+* will ensure that Team Wall Street will email you with timely updates and information that you can't afford to miss. This is a must for anyone who cannot spend all day searching the web for time-sensitive information.

IQ PAGER

IQ Pager is a paging system which beeps you as events and announcements are made on Wall Street. The key to the stock market is timing. Especially when you're trading in options, you need up to the minute (or second) information. However, most investors cannot afford to sit at a computer all day looking for news. We recognized need this and came up with an incredible and innovative solution—*IQ Pager*. You'll receive information such as major stock split announcements, earnings surprises, or any other news that will impact the market.

This new product is selling like crazy. Just imagine sitting in a meeting during the day and having the pager go off! Within minutes and sometimes before it hits the news wire you could know about the stock split. Two hundred characters of information show up on the pager, so it gives you enough to get you at least involved in a timely manner. We don't make any claims that we get every stock split or every piece of good news announced out there, but we sure get a lot of them. Right now the pagers are going off between five and 15 times a day!

ENTITY INTEGRATION

POWER OF NEVADA CORPORATIONS—A FREE CASSETTE
By Wade B. Cook
Nevada Corporations have secrecy, privacy, minimal taxes, no reciprocity with the IRS, and protection for shareholders, officers, and directors. This is a powerful seminar.

THE INCORPORATION HANDBOOK
By Wade B. Cook
Incorporation made easy! This handbook tells you who, why, and, most importantly, how to incorporate. Included are samples of the forms you will use when you incorporate, as well as a step-by-step guide from the experts.

THE FINANCIAL FORTRESS HOME STUDY COURSE
By Wade B. Cook
This eight-part series is the last word in entity structuring. It goes far beyond mere financial planning or estate plan-

ning, and helps you structure your business and your affairs so that you can avoid the majority of taxes, retire rich, escape lawsuits, bequeath your assets to your heirs without government interference, and, in short, bomb proof your entire estate. There are six audio cassette seminars on tape, an entity structuring video, and a full kit of documents.

REAL ESTATE

INCOME STREAMS—A FREE CASSETTE
By Wade B. Cook
Learn to buy and sell real estate the Wade Cook way. This informative cassette will instruct you in building and operating your own real estate money machine.

REAL ESTATE MONEY MACHINE
By Wade B. Cook
Wade's first bestselling book reveals the secrets of Wade Cook's own system—the system he earned his first million from. This book teaches you how to make money regardless of the state of the economy. Wade's innovative concepts for investing in real estate not only avoid high interest rates, but avoid banks altogether.

HOW TO PICK UP FORECLOSURES
By Wade B. Cook
Do you want to become an expert money maker in real estate? This book will show you how to buy real estate at 60¢ on the dollar or less. You'll learn to find the house before the auction and purchase it with no bank financing—the easy way to millions in real estate. The market for foreclosures is a tremendous place to learn and prosper. *How To Pick Up Foreclosures* takes Wade's methods from *Real Estate Money Machine* and super charges them by applying the fantastic principles to already-discounted properties.

OWNER FINANCING

By Wade B. Cook

This is a short, but invaluable, booklet you can give to sellers who hesitate to sell you their property using the owner financing method. Let this pamphlet convince both you and them. The special report, "*Why Sellers Should Take Monthly Payments*," is included for free!

REAL ESTATE FOR REAL PEOPLE

By Wade B. Cook

A priceless, comprehensive overview of real estate investing. This book teaches you how to buy the right property for the right price, at the right time. Wade Cook explains all of the strategies you'll need, and gives you twenty reasons why you should start investing in real estate today. Learn how to retire rich with real estate, and have fun doing it!

101 WAYS TO BUY REAL ESTATE WITHOUT CASH

By Wade B. Cook

Wade Cook has personally achieved success after success in real estate. *101 Ways to Buy Real Estate Without Cash* fills the gap left by other authors who have given all the ingredients but not the whole recipe for real estate investing. This is the book for the investor who wants innovative and practical methods for buying real estate with little or no money down.

PAPER TIGERS

By Wade B. Cook

Wade Cook's my personal introduction to the art of buying and selling real estate. In this set of six cassettes, Wade shares his inside secrets to establishing a cash flow business with real estate investments. You will learn how to find discounted second mortgages, find second mortgage notes and make them better, as well as how to receive six times your money back while structuring your business to attract investors and give you the income you desire. Also included is a manual filled with sample forms, letters, and agreements.

When you buy *Paper Tigers*, you'll also receive *Paper Chase* for free. *Paper Chase* holds the most important tools you need to make deals happen. Wde created these powerful tapes as a handout tool you can lend to potential investors or home owners to help educate them about how this amazing cash flow system works for them. Your cash flow asset base will profit as you use this incredible tool over and over again.

LEGAL FORMS
By Wade B. Cook

This collection of pertinent forms contains numerous legal forms used in real estate transactions. These forms were selected by experienced investors, but are not intended to replace the advice of an attorney. However, they will provide essential forms for you to follow in your personal investing.

RECORD KEEPING SYSTEM
By Wade B. Cook

A complete tracking system for organizing all of the information on each of your properties. This system keeps track of everything from insurance policies to equity growth. You will know at a glance exactly where you stand with your investment properties and you will sleep better at night.

MONEY MACHINE I & II
By Wade B. Cook

Learn the benefits of buying, and more importantly, selling real estate. Now the system for creating and maintaining a real estate money machine is available in audiocassette form. Money Machine I & II teach the step-by-step cash flow formulas that made Wade Cook and thousands like him millions.

ASSORTED FINANCIAL WISDOM

MONEY MYSTERIES OF THE MILLIONAIRES—A
FREE CASSETTE

By Wade B. Cook

How to make money and keep it. This fantastic seminar shows you how to use Nevada Corporations, Living Trusts, Pension Plans, Charitable Remainder Trusts, and Family Limited Partnerships to protect your assets.

BUSINESS BUY THE BIBLE

By Wade B. Cook

Inspired by the Creator, the Bible truly is the authority for running the business of life. Throughout this book Wade provides you, the reader, with practical advice that helps you apply God's word to your life. Wade's goal is to teach people everywhere how to become wealthy so that they can lead their lives of service to God, their families, and others.

DON'T SET GOALS (THE OLD WAY)

By Wade B. Cook

BE-ing! Prioritize and get into action. It is more important to be moving in the right direction than to know where you already are. In this book Wade tells you how taking action and "paying the price" is more important than just simply making the decision to do something. Don't set the goals. Go out and simply get where you want to go!

BLUEPRINTS FOR SUCCESS (1998)

Contributors: Wade B. Cook, David Elliott, Keven Hart, Debbie Losse, Joel Black, Dan Wagner and Dave Wagner

Blueprints For Success is a compilation of chapters on building your wealth through your business and making your business function successfully. The chapters cover education and information gathering, choosing the best business for you from all the different types of business, and a variety of other skills necessary for becoming successful. Your business can't afford to miss out on these powerful insights!

HIGH PERFORMANCE BUSINESS STRATEGIES
By Wade B. Cook

Your business cannot succeed without *you*. This course will help *you* become successful so your company can succeed. It is a combination of two previous courses, formerly entitled Turbo-Charge Your Business and High-Octane Business Strategies. For years, Wade Cook and his staff have listened to people's questions and concerns. Because they know that problems are best solved by people who already know the ropes, Wade's staff wanted to help. They categorized the questions and came up with about 60 major areas of concern. Wade then went into the recording studio and dealt head on with these questions. What resulted is a comprehensive collection of knowledge to get you started quickly.

WEALTH 101 (1997)
By Wade B. Cook

This incredible book brings you 101 strategies for wealth creation and protection that you can't afford to miss. Front to back, it is packed full of tips and tricks to supercharge your financial health. If you need to generate more cash flow, this book shows you how through several various avenues. If you are already wealthy, this is the book that will show you strategy upon strategy for decreasing your tax liability and increasing your peace of mind through liability protection.

UNLIMITED WEALTH AUDIO SET
By Wade B. Cook

Unlimited Wealth is the "University of Money-Making Ideas" home study course that helps you improve your money's personality. The heart and soul of this seminar is to make more money, pay fewer taxes, and keep more for your retirement and family. This cassette series contains the great ideas from **Wealth 101** on tape, so you can listen to them whenever you want.

RETIREMENT PROSPERITY

By Wade B. Cook

Take that IRA money now sitting idle and invest it in ways that generate you bigger, better, and quicker returns. This four audiotape set walks you through a system of using a self directed IRA to create phenomenal profits, virtually tax free! This is one of the most complete systems for IRA investing ever created.

TRAVEL AGENT INFORMATION

By John Childers

The only sensible solution for the frequent traveler. This kit includes all of the information and training you need to be an outside travel agent for a stable company. There are no hassles, no requirements, no forms or restriction, just all the benefits of travelling for substantially less *every time.*

COOK UNIVERSITY:

People enroll in **Cook University** for a variety of reasons. Usually they are a little discontented with where they are— their job is not working, their business is not producing the kind of income they want, or they definitely see that they need more income to prepare for a better retirement. That's where **Cook University** comes in. As you try to live the American Dream, in the life-style you want, we stand by ready to assist you make the dream your reality.

The backbone of the one-year program is the Money Machine concept—as applied to your business, to stock investments, or to real estate. Although there are many, many other forms of investing in real estate, there are really only three that work: the Money Machine method, buying second mortgages, and lease options. Of these three, the Money Machine stands head and shoulders above the rest.

It is difficult to explain **Cook University** in only a few words. It is so unique, innovative and creative that it literally stands alone. But then, what would you expect from Wade Cook? Something common and ordinary? Never! Wade and his staff always go out of their way to provide you with useful, tried-and-true strategies that create real wealth.

We are embarking on an unprecedented voyage and want you to come along. If you choose to make this important decision in your life, you could also be invited to share your successes in a series of books called *Blueprints For Success* (more volumes to come). Yes, it takes commitment. Yes, it takes drive. Add to this the help you'll receive by our hand-trained experts and you will enhance your asset base and increase your bottom line.

We want to encourage a lot of people to get in the program right away. You could save thousands of dollars, if you don't delay. Call right away! Class sizes are limited so each student gets personal attention.

Perpetual monthly income is waiting. We'll teach you how to achieve it. We'll show you how to make it. We'll watch over you while you're making it happen. Thank you for your consideration. We hope to see you in the program right away.

Cook University is designed to be an integral part of your educational life. We encourage you to call and find out more about this life changing program. The number is 1–800–872–7411. Ask for an enrollment director and begin your millionaire-training today!

The flagship course of **Cook University** is *Wealth Academy*. Fasten your seat belt and be prepared to take a drink from an asset protection and entity planning fire hydrant. This three day workshop defined the art of asset protection and tax reduction through entity engineering. Participants receive a flood of knowledge that until now has been available only through high-priced attorneys, few of whom specialize in more than one of the 57 subjects covered at the Wealth Academy. During these three days we will discuss, in depth and in detail, the six domestic entities which will protect you from lawsuits, taxes or other financial losses, and help you retire rich. You'll have a chance to completely structure your own affairs, with Nevada Corporations, Limited Partnerships, and all trusts: Charitable Remainder Trusts, Pension Plans, and Living Trusts. Protect your estate and pass it on to your loved ones while reducing your taxes to their lowest level. This is the flagship seminar of Wade Cook Seminars, Inc. We'll even discuss gold, Asset Protection Trusts and International Business Companies. This is definitely a seminar you need to attend. It is the only seminar that will cost you tens of thousands of dollars to miss!

IF YOU WANT TO BE WEALTHY, THIS IS THE PLACE TO BE

Classes Offered:

WALL STREET WORKSHOP

Presented by Wade B. Cook and Team Wall Street

The Wall Street Workshop teaches you how to make incredible money in all markets. It teaches you the tried-and-true strategies that have made hundreds of people wealthy.

NEXT STEP WORKSHOP
Presented by Wade B. Cook and Team Wall Street

An Advanced Wall Street Workshop designed to help those ready to take their trading to the next level and treat it as a business. This seminar is open only to graduates of the *Wall Street Workshop.*

YOUTH WALL STREET WORKKSHOP
Presented by Team Wall Street

We believe the best financial gift parents can give their child is the desire and knowledge to be self-sufficient, a team player, passionate, and willing to do "what it takes" to support themselves and their families. Whether he or she is starting from scratch or maintaining the family dynasty, the **Youth Wall Street Workshop** will give children the tools they need to get ahead.

The time has come. This three day seminar, designed for twelve to eighteen year olds, will cover basic and advanced investment strategies, vocabulary, business, entrepreneurship, options, attitudes, altruism, economics, communication, and more. In fact, it is many seminars rolled into one. This seminar is designed for teenagers, but if you know younger, capable students who could benefit from attending, they will not be turned away. We recognize that all of our adult students would love to attend, however, this workshop is just for teens. Give a child the gift of knowledge—financial knowledge to change their lives.

BUSINESS ENTITY SKILLS TRAINING (BEST)
Presented by Wade B. Cook and Team Wall Street

Learn about the five powerful entities you can use to protect your wealth and your family. Learn the secrets of asset protection, eliminate your fear of litigation, and minimize your taxes.

EXECUTIVE RETREAT

Presented by Wade B. Cook and Team Wall Street

Created especially for the individuals already owning or planning to establish Nevada Corporations, the Executive Retreat is a unique opportunity for corporate executives to participate in workshops geared toward streamlining operations and maximizing efficiency and impact.

REAL ESTATE WORKSHOP

Presented by Wade B. Cook and Team Main Street

This new experiential workshop is a two day "hitting the streets," finding, evaluating, buying, and selling the properties, that will make Real Estate investing come alive! Learn what to look for, what to offer, and how to make $5,000 by Friday, without using one cent of your own money. Learn the strategies of "cooking" properties that allows independent retirement, with a large monthly cash flow. Wade made his first fortune in real estate, and his methods have revolutionized the real estate industry. Learn from the master and from Team Main Street, a few handpicked students and instructors who have even outdone the master! This Real Estate Event is not to be missed.

ABBREVIATIONS

AGI .... Adjusted Gross Income

CD .... Certificate of Deposit

CPA .... Certified Public Accountant

CRAT .... Charitable Remainder Annuity Trust

CRT .... Charitable Remainder Trust

CRUT ...... Charitable Remainder Unitrust

ERISA ...... Employee Retirement Income Security Act of 1974

FICA .... Federal Insurance Contributions Act

FIFO .... First In First Out

GAAP .... Generally Accepted Accounting Principles

GIC .... Guaranteed Investment Contract

GST .... Generation Skipping Trust

HUD .... Department of Housing and Urban Development

IRC .... Internal Revenue Code

IRS .... Internal Revenue Service

IRA .... Individual Retirement Account

LIFO .... Last In First Out

NOL .... Net Operating Loss

QTIP .... Qualified Terminable Interest Property Trust

REIT .... Real Estate Investment Trust

SEP-IRA ... Simplified Employee Pension Plan - Individual Retirement Account

UCC .... Uniform Commercial Code

UGMA ..... Uniform Gift to Minors Act

Glossary

A-B Trust

A trust which combines the A format, giving everything to your spouse, and the B format, giving the maximum of $600,000 to the children, and allows you to retain control of your money, even after you have died.

ABQD Trust

A trust which combines the A-B Trust and a QTIP Trust. This trust is especially important if you have minor children.

Adjusted Gross Income

Income on which an individual computes federal income tax. Adjusted gross income is determined by subtracting from gross income any unreimbursed business expenses and other allowable adjustments—for example Individual Retirement Accounts (with exceptions outlined in the Tax reform Act of 1986), SEP and KEOGH payments, and alimony payments. Adjusted gross income is the individual's or couple's income before itemized deductions for such items as medical expenses, state and local income taxes, and real estate taxes.

Annuities

Form of contract sold by life insurance companies that guarantees a fixed or variable payment to the annuitant at some future time, usually retirement. In a fixed annuity the amount will ultimately be paid out in regular installments varying only with the payout method elected. In a variable annuity, the payout is based on a guaranteed number of units, unit values and payments depend on the value of the underlying investments. All capital in the annuity grows tax-deferred. Key considerations when buying an annuity are the financial soundness of the past, and the level of fees and commissions paid to salesmen.

ASSET

Anything having commercial or exchange value that is owned by a business, institution, or individual.

ASSIGN

To sign a document transferring ownership from one party to another. Ownership can be in a number of forms, including tangible property, rights (usually arising out of contracts), or the right to transfer ownership at some later time. The party who assigns is called the *assignor* and the party who receives the transfer of title—the assignment—is the *assignee*.

AUDIT, TAX

An audit by the Internal Revenue Service (IRS), or state or local tax collecting agency, to determine if a taxpayer paid the correct amount of tax. Returns will be chosen for audits if they have suspiciously high claims for deductions or credits, or if reported income is suspicious, or if computer matching of income uncovers discrepancies. Audits may be done on a relatively superficial level, or in great depth. If the auditor finds a tax deficiency, the taxpayer may have to pay back-taxes, as well as interest and penalties. The taxpayer does have the right of appeal through the IRS appeals process and, if warranted, to the U. S. Tax Court and even the U. S. Supreme Court.

BYPASS TRUST

Agreement allowing parents to pass assets on to their children to reduce estate taxes. The trust must be made irrevocable, meaning that the terms can never be changed. Assets put in such a trust usually exceed the amount that children and other heirs can receive tax-free at a parent's death. Under the 1981 Tax Act, this amount reached $600,000 in 1987. Parents can arrange to receive income from the assets during their lifetimes and may even be able to touch the principal in case of dire need. One variation of a bypass trust is the qualified terminable interest property trust, or Q-TIP TRUST.

CAPITAL GAIN

The difference between an asset's purchase price and selling price, when the difference is positive. When the Tax Reform Act of 1986 was passed, the profit on a capital asset held six months was considered a long-term gain taxable at a lower rate. The 1986 law eliminated the differential between long-term capital gain and ordinary income rates. In 1991, capital gains were limited to 28%.

CASH FLOW

The pattern of cash income and expenditures, as of a company or person, and the resulting availability of cash.

CERTIFICATE OF DEPOSIT (CD)

Debt instrument issued by a bank that usually pays interest, institutional CDs are issued in denominations of $100,000 or more, and individual CDs start as low as $100. Maturities range from a few weeks to several years. Interest rates are set by competitive forces in the marketplace.

CERTIFIED PUBLIC ACCOUNTANT (CPA)

An accountant who has passed certain exams, achieved a certain amount of experience, reached a certain age, and met all other statutory and licensing requirements of the U. S. state where he or she works. In addition to accounting and auditing, CPAs prepare tax returns for corporations and individuals

CHARITABLE CONTRIBUTIONS

Contributions made to charitable organizations. Often these contributions are considered deductible by the IRS.

CHARITABLE REMAINDER ANNUITY TRUST

An IRREVOCABLE TRUST that allows one donation into the trust. Payouts are established and the asset passes to the charity upon the death of the donor.

CHARITABLE REMAINDER LEAD TRUST

An IRREVOCABLE TRUST that pays income to charity during the Grantor's life and the remainder passes to designated family members upon the grantor's death. This trust reduces estate taxes while enabling the family to retain control of the assets.

CHARITABLE REMAINDER TRUST

An IRREVOCABLE TRUST that pays income to one or more individuals until the Grantor's death, at which time the balance, which is tax free, passes to a designated charity. It is a popular tax-saving alternative for individuals who have no children or who are wealthy enough to benefit both children and charity.

CHARITABLE REMAINDER UNITRUST

An IRREVOCABLE TRUST that allows for an initial donation as well as subsequent donations. Payouts are established and the assets pass to the charity upon the death of the donor.

COMMON STOCK

Units of ownership of a public corporation. Owners typically are entitle to vote on the selection of directors and other important matters as well as to receive dividends on their holdings. In the event that a corporation is liquidated, the claims of secured and unsecured creditors and owners of bonds and preferred stock take precedence over the claims of those who own common stock. For the most part, however, common stock has more potential for appreciation.

CORPORATION

A legal entity, chartered by a U. S. state or by the federal government, and separate and distinct from the persons who own it. It is regarded by the courts as an artificial person; it may own property, incur debts, sue, or be sued. It has three chief distinguishing features: 1) limited liability; owners can lose only what they invest, 2) easy transfer of ownership through the sale of shares of stock, and 3) continuity of existence.

There are two types of corporations: 1) A *"C" Corporation* is a regular, ordinary corporation that is taxed on its profits and losses, and 2) An *"S" Corporation* is treated like a partnership, and all of the profits and losses are taxed through to the individual tax brackets of its respective owners.

CREDIT SHELTER TRUST

This is sometimes called a Bypass Trust. This is a trust set up to bypass the spouse's estate and make sure your whole $600,000 one-time exclusion passes on to your heirs.

DEDUCTION

Expense allowed by the Internal Revenue Service as a subtraction from adjusted gross income in arriving at a person's taxable income. Such deductions include some interest paid, state and local taxes, charitable contributions.

DEFINED BENEFIT PENSION PLAN

Plan that promises to pay a specified amount to each person who retires after a set number of years of service. Such plans pay no taxes on their investments. Employees contribute to them in some cases; in others, all contributions are made by the employer.

DEFINED CONTRIBUTION PENSION PLAN

Pension plan in which the level of contributions is fixed at a certain level, while benefits vary depending on the return from the investments. In some cases, such as 401(k) plans, employees make voluntary contributions into a tax-deferred account, which may or may not be matched by employers. Defined contribution pension plans, unlike defined benefit pension plans, give the employee options of where to invest the account, usually among stock, bond and money market accounts.

DIRECTORS, BOARD OF

A group of individuals elected, usually at an annual meeting, by the shareholders of a corporation and empowered to carry out certain tasks as spelled out in the corporation's charter. Directors meet several times a year and are paid for their services.

DIVIDEND

The distribution of earnings to shareholders, prorated by class of security and paid in the form of money, stock, scrip, or, rarely, company products or property. The amount is decided by the board of directors and is usually paid quarterly. Dividends must be declared as income in the year they are received. Mutual fund dividends are paid out of income, usually on a quarterly basis from the fund's investments. The tax on such dividends depends on whether the distributions resulted from capital gains, interest income, or dividends received by the fund.

DURABLE POWER OF ATTORNEY

A legal document by which a person with assets (the principal) appoints another person (the agent) to act on the principal's behalf, even if the principal becomes incompetent. If the power of attorney is not "durable," the agent's authority to act ends if the principal becomes incompetent. The agent's power to act for the principal may be broadly stated, allowing the agent to buy and sell securities, or narrowly stated to limit activity to selling a car.

EMPLOYMENT RETIREMENT INCOME SECURITY ACT (ERISA)

A 1974 law governing the operation of most private pension and benefit plans. The law eased pension eligibility rules, set up the Pension Benefit Guaranty Corporation, and established guidelines for the management of pension funds.

ESTATE TAX

Tax imposed by a state or the federal government on assets left to heirs in a will. Under the Economic Recovery Tax Act of 1981, there is no estate tax on transfer of property between spouses. An exclusion which began at $250,000 in 1982 and rose to $600,000 in 1987.

EXCLUSION

On a tax return, items that must be reported, but not taxed. For example, corporations are allowed to exclude 70% if dividends received from other domestic corporations. Gift tax rules allow donors to exclude up to $10,000 worth of gifts to donees annually.

EXTENSION, AUTOMATIC

The granting of more time for a taxpayer to file a tax return. By filing an IRS Form 4868 by the original due date of the tax return, a taxpayer can automatically extend his or her filing date by four months, though the tax payment (based on taxpayer's best estimate) is still due on the original filing date.

FEDERAL INSURANCE CONTRIBUTIONS ACT (FICA)

Commonly known as Social Security, the federal law requiring employers to withhold wages and make payments to a government trust fund providing retirement and other benefits.

FIDUCIARY

A person, company, or association holding assets in trust for a beneficiary. The fiduciary is charged with the responsibility of investing the money wisely for the beneficiary's benefit.

FIRST IN FIRST OUT (FIFO)

A method of accounting for inventory whereby, quite literally, the inventory is assumed to be sold in the chronological order in which it was purchased. In accounting for the purchase and sale of securities for tax purposes, FIFO is assumed by the IRS unless it is advised of the use of an alternative method.

401(K) PLAN

A plan whereby employees may elect, as an alternative to receiving taxable cash in the form of compensation or a bonus, to contribute pretax dollars to a qualified tax-deferred retirement plan. Elective deferrals are limited to about $9,000 a year (the amount is revised each year by the IRS based on inflation). 401(k) plans have become increasingly popular in recent years, in many cases supplanting traditional DEFINED BENEFIT PENSION PLANS. Employees favor them because they cut their tax bills in the year of contribution and their savings grow tax deferred until retirement. Companies favor these plans because they are less costly than traditional pension plans and also shift the responsibility for asset allocation to employees.

GENERAL PARTNER

1) One of two or more partners who are jointly and severally responsible for the debts of a partnership; 2) managing partner of a LIMITED PARTNERSHIP, who is responsible for the operations of the partnership and, ultimately, any debts taken on by the partnership. The general partner will pick the properties to be bought and will manage them. In return for these services, the general partner collects certain fees and often retains a percentage of ownership in the partnership.

GENERALLY ACCEPTED ACCOUNTING PRINCIPLES (GAAP)

The conventions, rules, and procedures that define accepted accounting practice, including broad guidelines as well as detailed procedures.

GENERATION SKIPPING TRUST (GST)

Arrangements whereby your principal goes into a trust when you die, and transfers to your grandchildren when your children die, but which provided income to your children while they live. Once a major tax loophole for the wealthy because taxes were payable only at your death and your grandchildren's death, now only $1 million can be transferred tax-free to the grandchildren. Otherwise, a special generation skipping tax—with rates equal to the maximum estate tax rate—applies to transfers to grandchildren, whether the gifts are direct or from a trust.

GIFTING OR GIFT SPLITTING

Dividing a gift into $10,000 pieces to avoid gift tax. For example, a husband and wife who want to give $20,000 to their child will give $10,000 each instead of $20,000 from one parent, so that no gift tax is due.

GUARANTEED INVESTMENT CONTRACT (GIC)

Contract between an insurance company and a corporate profit-sharing or pension plan that guarantees a specific rate of return on the invested capital over the life of the contract. Many defined contribution plans, such as 401(k) plans offer guaranteed investment contracts as investment options to employees.

HOUSING AND URBAN DEVELOPMENT, DEPARTMENT OF (HUD)

A cabinet-level federal agency, founded in 1965, which is responsible for stimulating housing development in the United

States. HUD has several programs to subsidize low- and moderate-income housing and urban renewal projects, often through loan guarantees.

INDIVIDUAL RETIREMENT ACCOUNT (IRA)

Personal, tax-deferred, retirement account that an employed person can set up with deposits limited to $2,000 per year ($4,000 for a couple when both work, or $2,250 for a couple when one works and the other's income is $250 or less.)

INTERNAL REVENUE CODE (IRC)

Blanket terms for complexity of statutes comprising the federal tax law.

INTERNAL REVENUE SERVICE (IRS)

U. S. agency charged with collecting nearly all federal taxes, including personal and corporate income taxes, social security taxes, and excise and gift taxes. Major exceptions include taxes having to do with alcohol, tobacco, firearms, and explosives, and customs duties and tariffs. The IRS administers the rules and regulations that are the responsibility of the U. S. Department of the Treasury and investigates and prosecutes (through the U. S. Tax Court) tax illegalities.

IRREVOCABLE

Something done that cannot legally be undone, such as an IRREVOCABLE TRUST.

JOINT TENANCY OR TENANCY IN COMMON

Ownership of real or personal property by two or more persons in which ownership at the death of one co-owner is part of the owner's disposable estate, and does not pass to the co-owner(s). There is no limit to the number of persons who can acquire property as joint tenants/tenants in common, and those persons could be, but need not be married to each other.

KEOGH PLAN

A tax-deferred pension account designated for employees of unincorporated businesses or for persons who are self-employed (either full-time or part-time). As of 1995, eligible people could contribute up to 25% of earned income, up to a maximum of $30,000. Like the INDIVIDUAL RETIREMENT ACCOUNT (IRA), the Keogh plan allows all investment earnings to grow tax deferred until capital is withdrawn, as early as $59^1/_2$ and starting no later than age $70^1/_2$. The Keogh plan was established by Congress in 1962 and was expanded in 1976 and again in 1981 as part of the Economic Recovery Tax Act.

LAST IN FIRST OUT (LIFO)

A method of accounting for inventory that ties the cost of goods sold to the cost of the most recent purchases.

LIABILITY

The claim on the assets of a company or individual—excluding ownership equity. Characteristics: 1) it represents a transfer of assets or services at a specified or determinable date. 2) The firm or individual has little or no discretion to avoid the transfer. 3) The event causing the obligation has already occurred.

LIVING TRUST ALSO CALLED INTER VIVOS TRUST

A trust established between living persons-for instance, between father and child.

MONEY PURCHASE PLAN

A program for buying a pension annuity that provides for specified, regular payments, usually based on salary.

MUNICIPAL BOND

The debt obligation of a state or local government entity. The funds may support general governmental needs or special projects. Prior to the Tax Reform Act of 1986, the terms *mu-*

nicipal and *tax-exempt* were synonymous, since virtually all municipal obligations were exempt from federal income taxes and most from state and local income taxes, at least in the state of issue. The 1986 Act, however, divided municipals into two board groups: 1) PUBLIC PURPOSE BONDS, which remain tax-exempt and can be issued without limitation, and 2) PRIVATE PURPOSE BONDS, which are taxable unless specifically exempted. The tax distinction between public and private purpose is based on the percentage extent to which the bonds benefit private parties; if a tax-exempt public purpose bond involves more than 10% benefit to private parties, it is taxable.

There are two types of MUNICIPAL BONDS: 1) *Performance Bonds* which have collateral and a specific structure as a payback source; and 2) *General Revenue Bonds* which are against the city in general.

MUTUAL FUND

Fund operated by an investment company that raises money from shareholders and invests it in stocks, bonds, options, futures, currencies, or money market securities. These funds offer investors the advantages of diversification and professional management. A management fee is charged for these services, typically between 0.5 and 2% of assets per year.

NET OPERATING LOSS (NOL)

A tax term for the excess of business expenses over income in a tax year. Under tax loss carryback, carryforward provisions, NOLs can (if desired) be carried back two years and forward 20 years.

NEVADA CORPORATION

A business or company incorporated under the laws of the State of Nevada. No corporate tax, no stock transfer tax, no succession tax, and no franchise tax, no reciprocity with the IRS, no minimum capital requirement to start up a corporation, as well as the protection of the officers and directors of the company from being sued for the activities of the company make Nevada one of the best states for incorporating.

NON-VOTING RIGHTS

Shares in a corporation that do not entitle the shareholder to voting or proxy rights.

OWNER

The person who has ownership or title to property.

PARTNERSHIP

A contract between two or more people in a joint business who agree to pool their funds and talents and share in the profits and losses of the enterprise. Limited partnerships are also sold to investors by brokerage firms, financial planners, and other registered representatives. These partnerships may be either public (meaning that a large number of investors will participate and the partnership's plans must be filed with the Securities and Exchange Commission) or private (meaning that only a limited number of investors may participate and the plan need not be filed with the SEC). Some partnerships are oriented towards offering tax advantages and capital gains to limited partners, while others are designed to provide mostly income and some capital gains.

PENSION PLAN

A plan which provides replacement for salary when a person is no longer working. In the case of a DEFINED BENEFIT PENSION PLAN, the employer or union contributes to the plan, which pays a predetermined benefit for the rest of the employee's life based on length of service and salary. Payments may be made either directly or through an annuity. Pension payments are taxable income to recipients in the year received. The employer or union has fiduciary responsibility to invest the pension funds in stocks, bonds, real estate, and other assets; earn a satisfactory rate of return; and make payments to retired workers. Pension funds holding trillions of dollars are one of the largest investment forces in the stock, bond, and real estate markets. If the employer defaults, pension plan payments are usually guaranteed by the Pension Benefit Guaranty Corporation (PBGC).

POOLED INCOME FUND

An arrangement wherein you put your donations into a trust controlled by someone else. Your assets are pooled with others' assets. You receive your personal share of income.

POUR OVER WILL

A document included in a LIVING TRUST, usually one page long with notary endorsement on the back establishing that anything which has not been put into the trust will be poured into the trust upon your death.

POWER OF ATTORNEY

A written document that authorizes a particular person to perform certain acts on behalf of the one signing the document. The document, which must be witnessed by a notary public or some other public officer, may bestow either *full power of attorney* or *limited power of attorney*. It becomes void upon the death of the signer.

PROBATE

A judicial process whereby the will of a deceased person is presented to a court and an executor or administrator is appointed to carry out the will's instructions.

PROFIT SHARING PLAN

An agreement between a corporation and its employees that allows the employees to share in company profits. Annual contributions are made by the company, when it has profits, to a profit-sharing account for each employee, either in cash or in a deferred plan, which may be invested in stocks, bonds, or cash equivalents. The funds in a profit-sharing account generally accumulate, tax deferred, until the employee retires or leaves the company. Because corporate profit-sharing plans have custody over billions of dollars, they are major institutional investors in the stock and bond markets.

PUBLICLY HELD COMPANY

A company with shares outstanding that are held by public investors. A company converts from a privately held firm to a publicly held one through an initial public offering of stock.

QUALIFIED TERMINABLE INTEREST PROPERTY (QTIP)

Allows assets to be transferred between spouses. The grantor of a QTIP trust directs income from the assets to his or her spouse for life but has the power to distribute the assets upon the death of the spouse. Such trusts qualify the grantor for the unlimited marital deduction if the spouse should die first. A QTIP trust is often used to provide for the welfare of a spouse while keeping the assets out of the estate of another (such as a future marriage partner) if the grantor dies first.

QUITCLAIM DEED

A deed which conveys only what present interest a person may have in a particular property without making any representations or warranties of title. Such a deed is useful in clearing up doubtful claims such as possible dower rights or disputed liens. A person giving a quitclaim deed releases and waives all present rights, and if the grantor has good and merchantable title, this is what is conveyed. If the grantor actually has no interest in the property, no interest is conveyed. However, if the grantor later acquires good title to the property previously conveyed by a quitclaim, the grantor keeps it; it is not automatically passed on to the grantee.

REAL ESTATE INVESTMENT TRUST (REIT)

A company, usually traded publicly, that manages a portfolio of real estate to earn profits for shareholders. Patterned after investment companies, REITs make investments in a diverse array of real estate such as shopping centers, medical facilities, nursing homes, office buildings, apartment complexes, industrial warehouses, and hotels. To avoid taxation at the corporate level, 75% or more of the REIT's income must be from real property and 95% of its net earnings must be distributed to shareholders annually. Because REITs must distribute most of their earnings, they tend to pay high yields of 5 to 10% or more.

ROLLOVER

The movement of funds from one investment to another. For instance, an INDIVIDUAL RETIREMENT ACCOUNT may be rolled over when a person retires into an ANNUITY or other form of pension plan payout system. When a BOND or CERTIFICATE OF DEPOSIT matures, the funds may be rolled over into another bond or certificate of deposit. The proceeds from the sale of a house may be rolled over into the purchase of another house within two years without tax penalty. A stock may be sold and proceeds rolled over into the same stock, establishing a different cost basis for the shareholder.

SECTION 179

Section 179 of the Internal Revenue Code (IRC) deals with the amount businesses can immediately deduct on equipment purchases. Sometimes Section 179 is referred to as "asset expensing."

SELF-TRUSTEED PENSION PLAN

A pension plan or account wherein you are the administrator and trustee of your funds, not a brokerage house.

SHAREHOLDER

The owner of one or more shares of stock in a corporation.

SILENT PARTNER

1) Limited partner is a direct participation program, such as real estate and oil and gas limited partnerships, in

which cash flow and tax benefits are passed directly through to shareholders. Such partners are called silent because, unlike general partners, they have no direct role in the management and no liability beyond their individual investment; and 2) general partner is a business who has no role in management but represents a sharing of the investment and liability. Silent partners of this type are often found in family businesses, where the intent is to distribute tax liability.

SIMPLIFIED EMPLOYEE PENSION PLAN—INDIVIDUAL RETIREMENT ACCOUNT (SEP-IRA)

A pension plan in which both the employee and the employer contribute to an IRA. Under the Tax Reform Act of 1986, employees (except those participating in SEPs of state or local governments) may elect to have employer contributions made to the SEP or paid to the employee in cash as with cash or deferred arrangements (401(k) plans).

SINE QUA NON

An essential element or condition.

SOLE PROPRIETORSHIP

An unincorporated business owned by a single person. The individual proprietor has the right to all the profits from the business and also has responsibility for all the firm's liabilities.

SPENDTHRIFT TRUST

A simple trust created to hold assets if you are worried about a certain child wasting money, or if you are worried that potential creditors could attach your assets (or those directly owned by your children), or if you are worried about one of your children getting a divorce.

STOCKHOLDER

An individual or organization with an ownership position in a corporation; also called a shareholder. Stockholders must own at least one share, and their ownership is confirmed by either a stock certificate or a record by their broker, if shares are in the broker's custody.

SUBCHAPTER S

The section of the Internal Revenue Code giving a corporation that has 35 or fewer shareholders and meets certain other requirements the option of being taxed as if it were a partnership. Thus, a small corporation can distribute its income directly to shareholders and avoid the corporate income tax while enjoying the other advantages of the corporate form. These companies are also known as S Corporations, tax-option corporations, or small business corporations.

TAX RATE

The percentage of tax to be paid on a certain level of income. The United States uses a system of marginal tax rates, meaning that the rates rise with taxable income. The top rate is paid only on the portion of income over the threshold. Currently, the federal government has four tax rates 15, 28, 31 and 36%. There is also a 10% surtax on married couples filing jointly reporting taxable incomes of more than $250,000 or married couples filing separately with taxable incomes of more than $125,000. This creates an effective fifth tax rate of 39.6%.

TRANSFER

The exchange of ownership of property from one party to another. For example, a piece of real estate may be transferred from seller to buyer through the execution of a sales contract. Securities and mutual funds are typically transferred through a transfer agent, who electronically switches ownership of the securities.

TRUST

A fiduciary relationship in which a person, called a trustee, holds title to property for the benefit of another person, called a beneficiary. The agreement that establishes the trust, contains its provisions, and sets forth the powers of the trustee is called the trust indenture. The person creating the trust is called the creator, settlor, grantor, or donor; the property itself is called the corpus, trust res, trust fund, or trust estate, which is distinguished from any income earned by it. If the trust is created while the donor is living, it is called a LIVING TRUST or INTER VIVOS TRUST. A trust created by a will is called a testamentary trust. The trustee is usually charged with investing trust property productively and, unless specifically limited, can sell, mortgage, or lease the property as he or she deems warranted.

Trustee

A person or bank named in a trust to hold the legal title to property to administer it for a beneficiary.

Trustor

The person creating a trust. Also called a creator, settlor, grantor or donor.

Uniform Commercial Code (UCC)

The legal code adopted by most states that codifies various laws dealing with commercial transactions, primarily those involving the sale of goods, both tangible and intangible, and secured transactions. It was drafted by the National Conference of Commissioners of Uniform State Laws and covers bank deposits, bankruptcy, commercial letters of credit, commercial paper, warranties, and other commercial activities.

Uniform Gift to Minors Act (UGMA)

Enacted to provide a simple way to transfer property to a minor without the complications of a formal trust, and without the restrictions applicable to the guardianship of a minor's property. In many states, gifts under the UMGA can be made both by lifetime gift and by the donor's will. Lifetime UMGA gifts qualify for the $10,000 annual gift tax exclusion. A UGMA property is managed by a custodian, who is appointed by the donor. If the donor names him/herself as custodian, and if the donor-custodian dies before the property is turned over to the minor, the value of the custodial property at the donor-custodian's death is included in the donor-custodian's taxable estate, even though the property belongs to the minor from the instant the UGMA gift is made. The custodial property must be turned over to the minor when the minor attains the age specified in the UGMA law of the state under which the gift is made.

VOTING RIGHT

The right attending the ownership of most common stock to vote in person or by proxy on corporate resolutions and the election of directors.

WARRANTY DEED

A type of deed used to convey real property in which the grantor makes formal assurance as to the quality of title to the property. Warranty deeds, both general and special, are commonly used to convey real estate.

WILL

A document, also called a testament, that, when signed and witnessed, gives legal effect to the wishes of a person, called a testator, with respect to disposal of property upon death.

WRITE OFF

The charging of an asset amount to expense or loss. The effect of a write-off is to reduce or eliminate the value of the asset and reduce profits.

ZERO COUPON BONDS

A municipal bond which has no interest payout until a period some time in the future. All the gain and interest paid out is tax free.

Index

A

annuities 11,80
audits 46-48

B

bonds
    college 81
    EE savings.. 81
    general revenue 9
    municipal 8-11
    performance... 9
    zero coupon 10,149
business
    buying/selling 36
    deductions 25,
    ownership .... xvi, 73-74
                                          6

C

capital gains 86
case study #1 193
case study #2 198
case study #3 203
cash-to-asset-to-cash 73
Charitable Remainder Trust (see trusts)
college tuition 81
controlled groups 95
corporations 17, 46, 92, 93, 175, 183, 184
    and Living Trusts 96, 100, 176
    compared to FLP 162-166
    control 96
    deductions 24, 44
    estate planning 127-128
    Nevada corporations 97-99
    shareholders 94
    year-ends 102-107
CPAs... xxiv

D

deductions 25
    business/non-business 44
    intangibles 38
    losses.. 29
    tax ....xviii, 25
Defined Benefit Plan 112
Defined Contribution Plan 112
diversification.. 4, 77
dividends 78, 93
double taxation (see taxation)
durable power of attorney 140

E

EE savings bonds (see bonds)
entities
    corporations.. 46, 93, 94-107
    diversification 4, 77
    Family Limited Partnership 151-156, 162-166, 181
    integration ....xx, 178-187
    Living Trust (see Living Trusts)
    ownership 87-90
    Pension Plan 109-111, 118-121
    Rule A 88
    Rule B 89
ERISA Rule 404 (C) 125
Exclusion Rule (70%) 7, 78

F

Family Limited Partnership (see partnership)
financial structuring (also see structuring) xx
fully funded 141

G

general annuity Income (see income)
generation skipping trust (see trusts)
gifting 147-151
general partner 150, 154-166

I

income
    active/passive 27, 86
    allocating 12
    business/non business 45
    earned 27
    general annuity 11
    low income housing credits 31-36
    median family 33
    splitting 20
installment sales 55-59
investing
    angles 76-78
    aspects/formats 91
    stock market 76-78
    with annuities 80
IRA 110, 115

J

joint tenancy 4, 143

L

law of leverage 75, 118
law suits 93-95
Living Trust (scc trusts)
low income housing credits 31-36

M

median family income (see income)
money purchase plan 116
municipal bonds (see bonds)

N

net operating loss 42-43
Nevada Corporations (see corporations)

O

ownership
    cash flow 87
    control 72, 87, 176

P

Partnership
    compared to corporations 162-166
    Family Limited 151-156, 162-166
    general partner 156, 162-164
    tax consequences 158, 164
Pension Plan
    401(k) 124-127
    advantages 118-122, 126
    control 122
    cost 117
    Defined Benefit Plan 112
    liquidity 119
    safety 121
    Money Purchase Plan 112
Pour Over Will 141
probate 131, 141
Profit Sharing Plan 112

Q

Q-TIP provision (see Living Trust)

R

real estate 27
retirement 25, 71, 124
refund, immediate 43
Rule A & B (see entities)

S

section 179 59-70
section 2701 126
sole proprietorships 92-93, 113

stepped up basis 145
stock market 76-78
strategies
    corporate 91-100
    tax 21-26
structuring .... xx, 2, 5
    financial .... xx, 2

T

tax brackets 83-85
    "C" corporation 18
    corporate vs. individual 19
    married filing jointly 16
    single 17
tax forms
    1040 schedule C 65-68
    1040X 46
    1041 124
    1045 .... 43, 44, 46
    1099 .... 47, 51
    1120 59
    1120X 46
    1127 51
    1138 46
    2120 55
    2210 48
    4562 69-70
    4868 51
    6252 .... 55, 57, 58
taxation xviii
    children 22-23
    corporate vs. individual 19-20
    credits 30-36
    deductions 25
    double 86
    family limited partnership 15
    liability 4, 51
    Pension Plan 112
    personal 7-8
    points 53-55
    write offs 11-12
trustee 173-174
trusts 167-174

Charitable Remainder (CRT) 168-171
    Charitable Lead (CLT) 171
    Charitable Remainder Annuity (CRAT) 171
    Charitable Remainder Unitrust (CRUT) 171
    Pure/Commonwealth (PT/CT) 172
Credit Shelter (CST) 174
Generation Skipping (GST) 139
Living Trust
    A-B Trust 137
    corporations and Living Trusts 175, 176
    durable power of attorney 140
    generation skipping trust 139
    lifetime exclusion 136
    Living Trust vs. wills 131-132
    Pour Over Will 141
    Q-TIP provision 138
Spendthrift (ST) 174

U

units 23, 154-161

W

wealth accumulation (stages) 71
write offs (see taxation)

Y

year-end
    corporate 102-107
    tax maneuvering 49-52

Z

zero coupon bonds (see bonds)
"zeroing out" 29